The Course Of Miracles

The Zen Teachings of Jesus

Peter Bernhard

Stellaazul-Verlag
published in Barcelona 2016, Spain
by Peter Bernahrd
ISBN: 978-1544759586
https://innerwisehealing.wordpress.com

Table of Contents

1. Intro

Jesus is still present. He appears on art prints and in the churches. He is part of our history and our culture. He is often mentioned, as if he is well known indeed. But at the same time he seems to be infinitely remote, separated from us by space and time, as if he was living in a different world, that is lost to us now or that we do not want to remember anymore. In this world we may think God was much closer to people than now. The closeness to God, which Jesus represents, makes many people afraid. They believe that their freedom depends on a distant God, who can only locate them when they call on him. On the contrary closeness to God is understood as slavery.

At the same time there is something else going on. There is a great longing for an ideal world, how it may have existed in the past, a time when the world was not yet broken into pieces like it is now. Some traditional figures like the Pope or the Dalai Lama embody the seeming security of the past and represent therefore high authority and hope. Jesus embodied many of these things also, like projections of all kind, fears, desires and also the real authority of a savior.

He is therefore still part of the public discourse, although the churches seem to have used up his message in a way. Many people have turned away from them, because their answers do not work for them anymore. Religion has been pushed into the background. I have been replaced by other attempts of solutions that embody the western ideal of freedom better. Today the public debate is determined by the promises of modern communications and electronics, as if the question of inner happiness or even of redemption has evaporated. When that inner happiness is sought, it is sought rarely with Jesus.

A huge market has opened up these days, offering salvation outside of traditional Christianity. Estern teachings like Zen have become popular in the west, but did not change society until now. There is a flood of new, old and mixed offerings that often promise a shortcut on the spiritual path. Fast food and dilettantism determine large parts of this esoteric market. Set pieces of all religions and traditions are offered in such an amount that it is unique in all of history. We know, however, many of these rites and techniques work only when they serve the purpose for which they were created. They were originally embedded in overall context, which was determined by both the tradition and the community and has often only local significance. In the stew of these parts, torn from the traditions of knowledge, can the western individual hardly find anything that brings back peace and joy.

At the end, the seekers could still not escape the demands of everyday life nor have they mastered them in a way which has refunded them the inner happiness that they so desperately seek. Few seekers manage to put together the appropriate mix of methods to grow in the right way or even find enlightenment. Most of them always run for new methods without ever arriving. Many seekers have become tired of this lonely hunt for redemption.

Some turn back to the traditional churches or other established religions. Some young people who are looking for quick and easy answers follow the call for war and self sacrifice. This shows the power of our spiritual longing as the secret force that drives our lives, whether we are hedonists, careerists, losers, mystics or religious fanatics. In all of us sleeps a dragon and this dragon is nothing more than the old longing for our origins. This force will shake our lives when it wakes up. Jesus is still part of this awakening. Outside of the churches, a new picture of Jesus was formed in the last forty years. This picture of Jesus not only could cry, but laugh and dance. We still do not know what Jesus has actually taught.

This may change, because we do know more about it now, than at any time since the death of the last apostle.

We will show that Jesus has surprising answers for all of us, which will be fully understood only in the future. These messages to mankind received in the 20th century and intended for the third millennium are from him. This Jesus teaches here in a radical manner, like the old Chinese Zen masters. He points relentlessly towards the things that stand between us and enlightenment and calls us for a reversal now. He leads in a sovereign manner way through the darkness to the light. We are talking about the *Course in Miracles*. This document is of unusual clarity and force like the old Zen-writings of Huang Po and others. Since it changes the thinking of the student, it also transforms the world in which he lives. That is the reason why it is not suitable for all beginners on the inner path, unless they feel irresistibly drawn to it. It would be better if one already has some experience in spiritual practice, like meditation, shamanic work, Jesus prayer or yoga, before one ventures into this work. Otherwise, he can easily lose the ground under his feet.

Following an inner inspiration, I have inserted some conversations here of Jesus with Lucifer and others.

2. The Historical Jesus

Who was this Jesus of Nazareth, that man of flesh and blood, who walked with his friends through Palestine two thousand years ago? We need to take a brief look at the former spiritual and political situation to get an idea of what was going on around him back then. In his time the political and religious climate in Palestine was very dense. The Romans had occupied the country, but gave the Jewish people some freedom in their religion. The occupiers for example decided not to set up the statues of their gods in Jerusalem, where the Jews had their invisible God Yahweh worshiped for centuries. The Romans still allowed the temple cult and the continued existence of the corresponding Jewish hierarchy. Inside and outside the official Jewish establishment there were many religious groups with which Jesus had to deal with. Some were partly fanatical opponents of the Roman occupation and ready for violence all the time like the Zealots. Others had completely turned away from the world and expected the imminent return of the Messiah, like the Essenes. Still others tried to find an arrangement with the system and the occupying powers in order to save as much as possible of their Jewish identity for the future, such as the Sadducees, the representatives of the Temple establishment and the Pharisees, the more popular and liberal rabbis and scholars, from whom today's Judaism has descended. What kind of relation had Jesus to these groups and was there any uniqueness in his position?

Jesus was not a theologian or a priest. There are stories in the Gospels that attempt to prove that Jesus was able to discuss in a way with the theologians, as if he were one of them. But when we have a closer look at the stories and sayings of Jesus, we can see that he was not interested in theological discourses at all. In his time it was fashion in the synagogues to have long disputes on each set of the Torah. Since each Hebrew letter holds an image, a number and a level of creation, one can easily lose himself in endless interpretations. Jesus however opposed any kind of literalism, which insisted on the strict observance of the law and was ultimately based on guilt and fear of God. He did not believe that scriptures were more important than the well being of a person. His stories should convey experiences and epiphanies and set individuals free. He questioned everything and invited into new ways of thinking. He stood outside the established priestly cast and was not an official rabbi, but acted as a lay preacher, which gave him the freedom to say and do what he really wanted, even if he risked his life in doing that.

Jesus was not a king's son or part of a political or religious establishment, though he was said to be part of the lineage of King David, as claimed repeatedly in the New Testament. This can be proven no longer after the destruction of the records in the fire of the temple in 65, but the oral tradition was certain about it. Jesus did descend from a poor craftsman and came from Galilee. This was an area in the north, which was contaminated by the Hellenistic culture and regarded as religiously unreliable by traditional Jews.

However, Jesus was not a liberal. He resisted a softening of the Jewish faith in favor of Hellenistic influences. He did not intend to abolish the law, but to fulfill it. This meant for him to put the essence of the law, the love of God, into action in benefit of the people. God's call to repentance into another life of peace with one another and creation was not disputable for him.

Jesus was an opponent of the orthodox Sadducees, the party of the spiritual establishment in Jerusalem who held outwards peace with the Romans and passed inward on a strict observance of the Sabbath peace and the many other laws of the Torah. For Jesus, there were other things more important than the temple cult. He criticized the Sadducees for their inhumanity, putting the law higher than human dignity. Jesus did not speak polemic against the Romans in the biblical canon. Appropriate speeches were not taken up by the writers of the gospels out of political calculation. Jesus was probably certain however that an uprising against the occupying forces would not do any good, but would turn everything into destruction. A riot was also against the commandment to love each other, he taught.

Jesus believed in an imminent radical change of the world by God's direct intervention and the establishment of his rule, like many other people did in his time, for example, the Essenes and the Zealots.

He denounced the injustice of the system, without calling for revolution. For him, all true change was caused by God. The individual should get ready for conversion and renewal in preparation of this happening. This consists in renouncing the ego and in trusting the spirit of God, who had promised to lead all followers home.

History has shown why Jesus thought as he did. The Zealots, the *dagger men,* tried to end the domination of the infidels by war. They instigated the first major Jewish revolt against the Romans in 66 AD, which led to the destruction of the temple in Jerusalem by Titus in 70 AD and the loss of over one million lives. This downfall was prophesied by Jesus and was experienced by people and disciples who had still known him. A few decades later, another Jewish revolt broke out in North Africa and Cyprus, also with hundreds of thousands dead and massacres on both sides. The last major battle of the Jews in Roman Palestine, called after their leader *Bar Kochba Revolt*, also ended in defeat and ended in the expulsion of the remaining Jewish population of the province of Palestine.

Since Jesus did not support the fight against the Romans, he was sitting between all chairs. He probably incurred the hatred of the nationalist zealots, who preferred to see him in their ranks as a charismatic speaker.

Jesus did not foster any retreat from the world as the Essenes did. They divided the world into light and darkness, seeing themselves clearly as the children of light.

But Jesus taught and lived in the midst of the world and did not hesitate to contact the Romans, sinners or collaborators, such as he hated tax collectors. Furthermore, he did not teach any asceticism. He drank wine and ate meat and joined the festivities and meals of the rich with his entourage.

Jesus, however, was anything but a son of the middle class. He seems to resemble more of a modern hippie. He did not work, was fed by his followers, and did not bother about religious laws. As we already said, Jesus did not teach a compromise when it came to the real things like God, as the Pharisees did in his opinion. They believed that they could accumulate merit before God and divide their loyalties between God and the secular authorities.

Jesus did not believe in any religion of laws like today's Orthodox Judaism, Islam and Hinduism still are. God was a living reality for him, whose claim to the people could not be limited by anything.

So what after all of these accruals made Jesus special? He preached the kingdom of God. It was something mysterious, luminous and new, that was touched by the prophets of Israel only a few times over the centuries. This Reign of God whose total breakthrough was imminent in the near future, was already palpable in his own presence and that was the one thing that made Jesus really unique. The so-called "eschatological expectation" he shared with many of his contemporaries, as we said, particularly the religious zealots who expected not only the salvation of the world, was also the divine punishment for the unbelievers.

There was something that went far beyond this expectation. It was the teaching of the faith in God in all aspects of life, a life out of the uncertainty of the moment. This life surrendered itself to God moment by moment by its defenselessness. It gave him the room for his guidance and opportunity to bless one with miracles.

Jesus was certain that God would help the people who depended on him only. He pulled God closer to the people, made him a confidant again, a privilege of a few prophets until then. It is sure that he referred to himself not as the Son of God or the Messiah. The confession of being the Son of God was revered to him in the light of the post-Easter experience. But on the other hand, Jesus spoke during his teaching period with such an inner authority, that it seemed to indicate that he knew the will of God exactly as it was. The healings he accomplished seemed to prove also that his power and his claim were justified. They were not just empty words. The title of the 'Savior' and 'Christ' was awarded him by the post-Easter community therefore on a twofold basis; his life on earth being completely unique and his resurrection, which was, attested by many, the basis for the Christian faith and all the writings of the New Testament.

Later, the threat of hell was put into Jesus' mouth, which has terrified a whole Christian era. In the Old Testament, such a gloomy outlook did not exist, as there had not been any belief in after-life at that time. But could Jesus really threaten people with hell *and* speak of a loving Father in Heaven? If these threats should make any sense within the context of his doctrine of God's love, it could only mean that by denying the voice of the Holy Spirit, one will stay out of heaven. Being caught in the wheel of rebirth was called hell by the knowing. In summary, we can say that Jesus spoke not about the things we can see with our eyes. He spoke of a sphere of consciousness in which an unconditional love exists, which has no opposite because it is all encompassing. This is difficult to understand on earth, because all earthly laws and habits are pointing in the opposite direction.

But for Jesus this kind of love made perfect sense, because only in it he saw a way out of bondage and the suffering in the world. He had become a little familiar with his earthly life and his intensions. We can see what a genius had came to earth by him with the Course. This work empowers everyone with the tools for his own inner growth.

There were some outstanding ambassadors and successors of the teachings of Jesus, such as Meister Eckhart in the 13th Century, John of the Cross in the 16th Century and Mary Baker Eddy in the 19th Century. But now we have a document in hand, we thought was lost forever, a book in which Jesus speaks to our time. This could be the most important message to humanity since the New Testament. Are we ready for it?

3. First Conversation of Jesus with Lucifer

On the road from Jerusalem to Jericho, by 140 AD,

Jesus was wrapped in dark cloth.

Lucifer was in the garb of a Roman officer.

L: "Where is now the kingdom of God you have prophesied? It's all gone down the drain. Jerusalem's temple is destroyed and your Christians are scattered to the four winds. Of the Jews, your people, we don't even speak."

J: "As I already foresaw. Even the stones have cried in my vision. It would have been better not to know the future. Even better it would have been if my people had listened to me."

L: "And the kingdom of God? Is it still coming? Did you not say that your disciples will see it coming? "

J: "The kingdom of God has come with my awakening. You know exactly what's going on, Lucifer."

L: "No, I do not see anything. Another time, you made an unfulfilled promise. You have not made any decision. You didn't join the liberals nor the fanatics nor the collaborators. You had danced at every wedding... The Jews fought at least. But your people just ran away and have been waiting for God or you to come back. But neither God nor you showed up again."

J: "For those who did not listen, the story may reach out into the future for a long time. For those however, who hear me, I'm forever there. You look at a world, which winds up in agony, because it believes in your thoughts. You think you're an advocate of the people, who needs to be defended against the love of God. But this is not so. Inside the heart of every one who walks on this earth, the kingdom of God still shines perfectly clear and untouched, even in you. I wanted everyone to remember, for the kingdom of my father has no end."

4. Salvation Without Sacrifice

The shared idea that "there must be another way" was a prerequisite for receiving the messages of Jesus for the third millennium. Two people had joined together in the search for a better way. They were Schucmen Helen and William Thetford, both professors in the Department of Medical Psychology at Columbia University in New York City. They had suffered from the stress and the rivalry in their fields, but also under their inadequate means for helping. They had searched seriously for an alternative. However, they were both scientists through and through and did not believe in spiritual things. When Helen's inner awareness woke up by vivid dreams and advance knowledge of important events, she panicked. Especially when the inner voice started to speak to her saying, "This is a course in miracles, please take notes!" The encouragement of Bill was needed to reassure her to start to write the material down. The course material Helen was given between 1965 and 1972 happened in an inner dictation which could be interrupted at any time and resume elsewhere. Meanwhile, she was in no trance, but in her normal waking state. The content of the material was deeply contrary to her scientific and atheistic beliefs. She remembered one moment oddly though that she had committed herself to the writing of this message a long time ago. Memories of events "before this lifetime" was the last thing she could accept. So she was about to destroy her writings and finish the listening after that inside. However, since she recognized the urgency of this endeavor, she agreed to cooperate further, but without knowing how much material would be given and how long it would take. It took seven years to receive the three books which this course consists of now.

This material contains the blueprint of the human spirit. If we apply it, our lives will change dramatically. There are no boundaries for the help it can provide us with. To understand it, we have to forget much of what we think we know and try to consider all things in a new way. The answer was not where we thought it might be; otherwise we would have found it long ago.

If we are really desperate, then we may ask ourselves if we were wrong, or if we had taken a wrong turn somewhere in our lives. And it is this question we should ask ourselves now, in case we spend our lives not in perfect love, but in deep peace and full of happiness yet. But who likes to admit a mistake? In most cases, we will justify our decisions, as long as we can, in order not be responsible. If we insist in being innocent, we must logically regard ourselves as victims of outside circumstances. In this way we have seemingly saved our innocence, but have also thrown away the power to determine our lives. Many spend lifetimes in this way because they believe they must escape responsibility for their failures at any cost. Why are we so afraid of responsibility and guilt?

Why is it so terrible to fail? And who could condemn us? These fears may have a cause but it must lie deeper than we suspect. Maybe they have to do with our buried and forgotten relationship with God. We do not want to think like the people of ancient times, who considered their soul as a vast ocean in which they could get lost or find their identity. We believe to have only a small ego, which is opposed to a vast universe that can only be protected by sophisticated techniques and safety precautions. What would happen if someone told us that we were wrong all the way and our opinions and judgments meant nothing? If we allowed this acknowledgement representing the message of the Course to be true for a moment, what would change? If we were wrong completely, then we would wander blindly through an obscured world and we would be pushed around by unknown forces. Does this sound a little familiar? Why then are we still alive? The author of the course says we sleep safely in heaven, while we are dreaming of danger and death. The course points out a way to safe dreams that ultimately will lead us to the awakening.

He promises it to open up a path, of which we didn't hear before, a path of glory, presenting a scenery of grandeur and vast vistas that open when one is proceeding further. But even in these prospects, where the radiance can reach incredible heights, what remains still behind all that is waiting for us at the path's end. This way leads towards love, but what love really is and what it can be for us, we will understand only little by little along the way and not completely until the very end.

The course tries to speak of things that are beyond our ability to grasp and even further he tries to train our thinking in such a way that we can reach a vision of another world.

The course was called by Sai Baba, an Indian avatar, the "Vedanta in the West." The Hindu Vedanta speaks of how the world had emerged from the Absolute, which laws determine the life here and what kind of yoga should be used for the different paths to liberation from the cycle of rebirth. Furthermore, the Vedanta teaches everyone that they can wake up from the dream of the world, once one recognizes his own perfection and in constant awareness.

The Course in Miracles does not agree with all of the Vedanta's teachings, especially not with the idea of this world arising from the inhaling and exhaling of Brahman/God. The Course is quite certain in saying that this world was not created by God and agrees herein with the western Gnostic tradition and Buddhism.

It speaks the language of the biblical story of salvation, though it reinterprets much of it. Where it is recognized as what it is, it changes the course of many spiritual shores, by demonstrating a direct path to God and also by claiming to contain a personal message of Jesus to our time and thus giving the world an insight into his thinking.

This Jesus wants to be a brother and a leader towards the awakening and finding inner peace in the world. In a time in which western Christianity is losing it's importance, the figure of the Nazarene returns in a form of a universal and uncompromising message that prompts everyone to take responsibility for the world and to wake up from the dream of time.

The course is asking each one of us, as Jesus did, when He asked his disciples two thousand years ago to change our way of thinking and thus our lives. But the belief in Jesus as Savior is not required here anymore, because Christ can take many forms and each one of us must ultimately be the redeemer of his own dream in order to be free.

The Course advises us to re invite Jesus back into our lives as companion and as friend. Although the Course freed his teachings from all ideas of sacrifice, it requires a sacrifice still. This one appears great indeed, even bigger than the one required by traditional Christian doctrine which was the letting go of all dreams of the things of this world as a goal in our lives and their exchange for something else, almost unknown, intangible, a state of mind called heaven. A sacrifice of this kind is already well known to us. Those who engage in a love relationship have to decide against all others, those who accept a job do miss all the other opportunities and those who do not decide for anything at all will end up with nothing. Therefore, any kind of decision we make seems to rob us of our imagined freedom we seem to have as long as we do not decide yet. The Course rejects this assumption. It says it requires only one decision to liberate us from our self-inflicted captivity. A decision for what? This decision is for the beautiful, true, and good as our real home.

What can we say about the belief in hell within the context of this Course? Even without the Course the belief in hell already dissipated in postmodern times since society has become aware that punishment rarely represents a help and hardly leads to improvement, but rather produces retreat into debt and projection. Projection means in modern Psychology and the Course that the mind sees its own surpressed emotions such as guilt, hate and lack of selfesteem in others and tries to attack this *shadow* in them. But there is also a growing recognition in modern psychology of our need for accepting our own responsibility for life. It is important for adolescents, for example, to be confronted with the consequences of their actions. The Course emphasizes that life on earth is an education process in itself. We can not escape it, which is a very sobering realization for us. The healing of our dark side can be done by honesty, shared love and prayers for help. In the language of the Course, will our prayers for help be answered with miracles if we have done our parts? The greatest miracle is the changing of our mind.

The church founded its religion on the idea of sacrifice, just as the Jews had done until the year 70, when their temple was destroyed during an uprising against the Romans. The Apostle Paul preached that Jesus died for the sins of the people. And somehow God seemed to have wanted this sacrifice. But this momentous hypothesis was not helpful in overcoming the fear of God. If Jesus had to die for the sins

23

of the people, they must have been real. And a real sin can not be forgiven, except by a magical, magical act. That's why Christianity threatens humankind with the Last Judgment, which will happen when God loses his patience and stretches out his avenging hand to throw all sinners into eternal fire.

The idea that blood must be shed in order for life to thrive, (as shown in the crucifixion), goes back to earlier times, when Mother Earth was still understood as a living goddess. The ancient people had noticed the stopping of the female menstruation during the pregnancy. They concluded the embryo must consume its mother's blood. So they inferred that Mother Earth needed blood for letting the next crop thrive. Therefore, they sacrificed plants, animals and even humans. In Judaism, the sacrifice of animals was understood as atonement for the sins of the people. The basic idea was, as we said, sin being real and someone had to pay for it. No one can escape the idea of sin, as long as he holds the world to be real, says the Course. And who can doubt the reality of the world, as long as he does not have a tool to see a different reality?

5. Acceptance of One's Innocence

In the Course Jesus gives the crucifixion another interpretation that is free of fear. Salvation was not been obtained by the crucifixion, but by the resurrection. The latter represented the overcoming of death and is the proof of the indestructible innocence of the children of God. The acceptance of the atonement, advocated by the Course again and again, is the acceptance of one's innocence and identity in God, to which Jesus awoke himself. This act of faith is available to any traditional Christian as well as to the students of the Course In Miracles. The experience of redemption already accomplished was given to Martin Luther in his *Tower Experience*. Why is this acceptance of our innocence so difficult for us, when it gives us back our freedom? Many of us have a much deeper investment in guilt than they can admit. It is the basis of our whole self identity. We do many things in our lives only to expiate for this original debt. If we try to be "good" or to make everything right or to be someone who earns a lot of recognition this is maybe the case. Many strive to release that guilt their entire life.

Where this feeling of guilt comes from, when it has not been implemented in us by religion? The Course states that in the deepest part of our psyche a burning love for God is hidden. This love is so strong that we would jump into heaven if we remembered it. This is a scary notion for many of us. That is why we have placed our deepest guilt on the top of this love, because when we created this dream, we already felt guilty in relation with God and therefore wanted to ensure that we never returned to heaven. In order to forestall the punishment of God, we created our own punishing God, the ego.

What is our deepest guilt then? It's the idea that each one individually has stolen himself and his part of the cosmic mind from God and thus destroyed the unity of heaven. That's why one believes somehow that God is after him. The reason why God has not found him yet can only be the seeming fact that there are so many of us. He may have found others but not me. The realization of one's innocence reverses this upside-down belief system and opens it for healing.

6. The Aim of the Change of Mind

The Course represents a perfectly coherent thought system as Jesus´ teaching always was, in which each part stands for the whole, in the same way as in a hologram or the universe. As mentioned earlier, this thought system can not be understood with the mind. The mind must learn to act in a different way. I have to step aside and to relax in order to allow the spirit to let the happy revelation of one's innocence and divine identity shine into the still awareness. The Course fosters this change by means of the exercises of the Workbook. This is a unique system of practice in a new thinking for our time. After the student has accomplished this transformation under the inner guidance of the Holy Spirit, he finds himself in a new world in which the concern for his life falls away because someone else is taking care of him. The deep inner conflict is taken from him. Since he no longer has to worry about his fate, he can begin to act without fear and to remember his dreams. Instead of denying his real passion in favor of enlightenment the student should give it to the Holy Spirit and allow him to use it for awakening. A conflict-free mind can serve God and humanity and can express its passion as a human being. Only the ego creates conflict, because it has no positive goals and does not know what joy is.

This Course achieves its goal of change of mind by placing complete forgiveness within the reach of human consciousness. The awareness of forgiveness being a decision is becoming more popular in today's psychology. The Course is actually based on this idea. Jesus had taught it two thousand years ago already. Furthermore, Jesus teaches that we can only remember God when we include our neighbor and ourselves in what we think God's identity is. The Course rejects therefore the idea, that God would be an objective entity, separated and opposed to His own creation. Most people who were raised as Christians have God imagined that way. They may felt sometimes observed by a third party during their childhood and their childish pranks. That was not really fun.

A probably true story of a little girl who grew up with her pious grandmother, who threatened her repeatedly with God, reported that this girl never wanted to go out in sunny weather and if, then only under a broad-brimmed hat, that God could not see her. We all have tried to hide away from this God. Most of us have developed strategies of self-defense to justify our failure to love more. We have played the role of a victim in order not to be responsible for our selves.

However, taking responsibility is the way back to our wholeness. But who dares to take this kind of responsibility, unless he was previously been assured that he is still innocent? God has better things to do than to count the failures of his children, partly because the concept of guilt does not exist in God's Spirit. Furthermore, why would he leave his children in an environment for which they have not been created and function poorly here?

7. Second Conversation Between Jesus and Lucifer

Venice Carnival 149., St. Mark's Square, Thursday night before Ash Wednesday, there are fireworks, wildly crying crazy people wearing masks, depraved young men forming human pyramids, dancing couples all dressed in gorgeous clothes. Lucifer is disguised as a devil, Jesus as a juggler.

L: "And all this is supposed to be a dream that will pass away like the foam of the sea, without a trace in the spirit of the Almighty?"

J: "Yeah, you say it. It passes like sea foam, without leaving a trace."

L: "And you say furthermore, all these people are gods? Parts of the expansion of the Almighty?"

J: "Yes, because there is no life except the Life of God."

L: "But it's nonsense to say that these people are still one with God. This is the paradise of the devil and I enjoy it. Even the heavens seem close to me in this frenzied party of love and lust. But tomorrow morning, when the people rise with heavy hangovers from their rumpled beds, I will strive diligently, to engage them into new searches for happiness, to keep them busy while your little voice will cry out to God in vain. They are so far from God as I am."

J: "You're right about the experience of the people and your own. But deep down inside you know the truth: Even though you have fallen since your rebellion against God from heaven into the depths and continue to fall and fall and fall, you are still not one inch away from the Source of all life, as those people either."

L: "You're a true Fool of God, Jesus. I do know you now for a while and you haven't changed yet. As the world did not either. Will you say the same thing even in some hundred years? "

J: "What is true must be forever true, no matter how high your illusions of inferno and despair pile up. Illusions can not add up, they remain meaningless, no matter in what amount of numbers they are presented. For the suffering of the people in the future I will shed many tears, that's true. And yet my trust in each of them remains. Everyone will make a different choice and come home where all tears are dried forever. I cannot take this decision away from anyone and not from you either, my friend. "

L: "If I only could believe this. But I still have enough to do. There are simply too many who are very content to listen to me. If you have all convinced of the return, and I can no longer bear the loneliness of the world, then maybe I'll even knock on heaven's door and call out for you, for I will probably need a friend then. I don't want to deal with Peter alone."

J: "Well let's see if I still remember you then..." also laughing.

L: "If not its also ok. I am used to dancing outside of heaven. And even eternal death does not scare me at all. What's bad about falling into non-existence and oblivion? For me that is eternal peace!"

8. Self-expansion is the Way God Creates

God creates only as himself and his self-expansion is the creation. Everything He created is forever and does not change although it continues to expand and to increase in joy. In other words, God has created us as part of Himself like all things, and nothing is outside of Him. God is Life and what lives is part of Him. Therefore did God not create the world, because Life is neither born nor dies. The expulsion from paradise in Genesis did so only happen in dreams, as Kabbalists and ancient Gnostics have taught for a long time. The Bible itself mentions that a deep sleep fell over Adam (1st Moses 2:21-22) and nowhere does it say that he awoke again. The Course says that God knows nothing of this world, but He is aware that some of his kids are not in peace, because they dream to be in the world. He therefore sent his Holy Spirit down to earth, as a guide back to Heaven. The Course asks each one to listen to the Holy Spirit and to be guided by him every day of his life. This Holy Spirit is nothing other than the united spirit of the Son of God Himself. And the Son of God is only one, just the one who is dreaming this dream and is reading this text now.

9. The Structure of the Course

The course consists of three books, the Textbook, the Workbook and the Teacher's Manual. The Textbook deals with the abstract and philosophical foundations of the Course. It starts with the summary of the entire teaching of the Course in the preamble: Nothing real can be threatened, nothing unreal exists, herein lies the peace of God. Those who have accepted these words as true and identified themselves with the Truth beyond appearances can jump straight onto heaven and do not need to read the rest of the Course. For the others the Textbook begins with the miracle principles. Miracles in the Course are not meant as an addition to the world of illusions. They stand instead for a collapse in the space-time continuum, which brings all who are involved nearer to salvation, and heal the feeling of lack which is based on error. A miracle is a moment of perfect communication and this is the way out of isolation towards salvation. If the world is released for a moment, out of control of the mind, it can be reconfigured. If all things fall into a new order the miracle is part of this change, as an opening or a solution that was inconceivable before.

9.1) The Playbook

In the Textbook (chapter 6) three stages of spiritual awakening are described.

The first step includes the prompt: To have, give all to all. Since the thinking of the world is based on the principle of having, such as the ownership of love, identity, knowledge, recognition and money, we must teach the contrary, if the transcendence of the world is our goal. To give oneself away, to serve the universe and all beings, has nothing to do with sacrifice. He who gives love learns that love is in him. He who gives attention realizes that he is not alone. He who gives of his time realizes that he is free of time. God has created his children *as* anything, but they have deprived themselves by their contraction of awareness. Therefore they must learn to expand again, to remember who they are and what they have. The Holy Spirit is the inner advisor who will only ask for things that can be done by the students without too much fear. The abolition of internal conflict is the goal. Spilled feelings will come up during this process of awakening. We are all full of anger when we begin to walk our way. This is the normal condition of man on earth. It is important not to identify with these feelings, but to allow them to rise following the breath up the spine until the crown. It is also important to not to believe one's own interpretations of those feelings. Feeling itself is an act of liberation. The thinking of the student will try to pull him back to the past though. The thoughts and interpretations must therefore be transcended in a gentle awareness.

The third statement is: Use your vigilance only on behalf of God and His kingdom. This statement allows you to perform the way that is outlined by this course, easier and easier, because the pain of entertaining thoughts of separation and fear will be less and less tolerable. Ultimately, the reality of the kingdom of heaven, which is already present in every spirit on earth, will shine away all foreign thoughts. This means specifically to refuse to indulge in fantasies of revenge and condemnation of any kind and to turn to the higher self instead, to restore peace. To be willing to do the will of God in every moment is the best way to preserve inner peace.

In the nineteenth chapter outlines the textbook over obstacles of peace. We are the visionaries of the world. If we want to see a world of peace, the peace of us needs to be extended outwards. This it will do by itself. But the peace will encounter obstacles that we we or others put in its way. We have done many things in order not to receive the peace of God, because we equate it with death or because we are afraid of God.

These answers go deeper than modern psychology has ventured until now. The first obstacle on the path to peace is the desire to get rid of it. We do not want peace, we prefer to keep our guilt, to which we hold unto instead. Guilt is the anchor which holds us in our comfort zone. We do not want peace, because it means tearing down the small wall between us and our brothers. And we want to keep a small part of the mind for ourselves. To completely forgive our brothers and sisters would mean for us to forego the privilege of private thoughts and even to give up the part of the mind we occupy and be washed into infinity.

Jesus says very clearly that we have to offer a home to the Holy Spirit in our minds in order to gain self-security. As long as we are looking for guilt in the world, we are living in a condemned world and will experience fear and terror. But we have the opportunity to send out the messengers of the Holy Spirit instead, to look for the smallest sign of love out there. If we do, we welcome the peace of God and we have overcome the first obstacle to Peace.

The next obstacle described in the course is the attraction of the body. Those who live on earth as a human being will usually identify themselves with living in a body and being a body. Give up this body in exchange for an infinite space full of light and peace, may be a scary idea for most of us. But Jesus asks precisely this: that we allow the inner peace to expand into the universe, and thus to be prepared to heaven in our awareness again. But we are not ready for it yet, otherwise we would not be here.

We believe that the sacrifice of the body and its pleasures is too much to ask of us as an exchange for something that we do not know and that frightens us by its size, depth and potential emptiness. Jesus emphasized that the loss of the body is not a loss at all but an end of limitation and pain. How can the peace move into us then? For the Course in Miracles, it is the holy relationship that makes this possible. A single individual can not accomplish it. The Philosophy of dialogue of Martin Buber, is close to this and reminds us, that we need each other for salvation today.

The third obstacle that peace must overcome in its expansion is the attraction of death. All who fear death are in fact, attracted to it. Death is seen as the secret savior of the inner conflict of humanity. He is the savior from the approach of light and Truth. Our brother can be the liberator of the attraction of death when he has been forgiven.

If we decide to see the true light of our neighbor rather than his physicality and his sins, all the dark shapes that we have made to keep us here, will stand up and summon us not to look into the light. The Course described these figures pictorially: The "holy" waxen face of death, the sweet allure of sin, and finally the ego itself, which we have sworn with blood never to betray it. And with the arrival of the light all that will disappear and will be forgotten.

 The fourth and final obstacle to peace is the fear of God himself, the craziest idea to which people are able to. God is for all beings in the universe without question the all loving source, protective and caring forever. To fear Him proves that one is trapped in the darkness of a crazy dream. Escape from this is not possible without assistance from the outside. Jesus makes no big deal out of the fear of God, because it is directly related to the three previous obstacles. If the attraction of death has lost its appeal and life is celebrated instead, the remembrance of God will dawn upon the mind.

The face of the brother who has been forgiven is the face of Christ. It is no longer stained with blood, as it seemed to be under the judgmental gaze of the ego, but in the reflection of the heaven's light. The fear that has raised this obstacle, dissolves, when the spirit remembers his yearning for love, which is greater than any wish for death. To overcome the last obstacle is the same as to forgive the neighbor; to forgive one completely means to change the whole world forever.

The world was depending on it from the beginning: Our mutual fear. Without this, it can not be a place of separated bodies anymore, and no bastion against heaven. The world will not be an attack on the unity of God and his creation anymore as the Course it describes. We need to lift the veil of ignorance for achieving liberation and we do that by looking at our brothers and sisters as a part of our selves, as sinless and unchanged since our creation by God. We are still as God created us and therefore there is nothing to fear. Without the fear of God, heaven will open its doors, whether we still walk on earth or vanish into invisibility.

The textbook contains many other ways, notes and reflections that illuminate the theme of awakening in different ways. For example, Jesus explains that he can not take the fear of the student away. Fear is subject to one's own responsibility and is a sign of listening to the wrong voice of the ego. Who listens to the voice of God will feel no fear. By this teaching, the textbook lays a great responsibility into the hands of the student. Thus, a kind of spirituality is taught that is more similar to Buddhism, where such self-responsibility is already familiar. In Christianity, however, the dependence on God was emphasized until now.

Even in the course, God-dependency is emphasized. Here salvation is based on the cooperation between the Holy Spirit and the student. This may not have been told in traditional Christianity, but it was always clear, that a Christian must recognize the redemption or at least believe in it, in order to gain it for himself. In the Catholic faith it is the good *deeds*, which is regarded as crucial in addition to the seven sacraments. In the Protestant church, it is the b*elief* in salvation and in the Course, it is the *decision for God* that causes the difference. Salvation is recognized in the Course, as in Protestantism, as having already happened. However, it is made clear that salvation must be lived in this life, in order to express and incorporate it. In order to experience salvation, certain requirements must be fulfilled, revolving around the theme of forgiveness. In traditional Christianity, redemption was achieved by the Jesus` crucifixion, who as we know, shed His blood for the sinners. In the Course, it was obtained by the resurrection of Jesus, because it proved that God's children are indestructible and that the ego is powerless.

9.2) The Workbook

The workbook follows the textbook, whose aim is to open our mind. The introduction of it says the goal is an all-encompassing training of the mind in a different perception of the world. The exercises will help to generalize the lessons, so that they will be equally applicable to things that one sees.

The training in true perception is different than the training in the world. True perception gained in connection with anything, is transferred to all things certainly. On the other hand, one exception held against true perception makes it accomplishment anywhere impossible.

This is a unique statement in the spiritual literature. The whole world, the whole universe is explained as a thing that has no exceptions. Thus, the holographic nature of the perception of the world is disclosed to which the workbook will lead. It consists of 365 lessons, each one for every day of the year.

The first lesson says that nothing we see means anything and the second lesson reveals to us that we have been given all the meaning we see in the world. Herein the Course teaches that we see no meaning in the world, which does not exist independently of us; we have projected all and held it up by further projection. We don't know the true meaning of the things we see. The visible things have been lifted into visibility by the desire for separation and objectivity.

If we choose we can receive a different meaning for all the things we see. The lesson 30 says that God is in all things we see, because God is in our mind. This lesson is a springboard for a visionary view of the world to which the Course is leading us. This vision is nothing else than the melting of all visible things into one holographic sight in which the unity of the Spirit is emphasized, rather than obscure like now.

As we said help these and other lessons to achieve the goal of the Course. A student of the Course will start usually after completing one year again with the lessons, although this is not explicitly asked for in the workbook.

9.3) The Teacher's Manual

The teacher's book answers to some of the common questions and needs of the student. Whoever undertakes to study this Course becomes a Teacher of God. In order to fulfill this function, he must learn to listen to the voice of the inner teacher, who is called the Holy Spirit. The acceptance of this all-encompassing spirit in our lives is the goal of the course. The real goal is the attainment of inner peace, which is obtained by complete forgiveness.

To be a teacher of God means to be in the service of Christ. This may include a personal relationship with Jesus or not, whose voice has given this Course after his testimony. What is crucial to the future Teachers of God is to consider the interests of others, separated from one's own. The idea that "there must be another way" is indeed the conclusion on which the Course was based. The course was based on two people united in the decision of a moment in this search for a better way, as we have already described. In the Teacher's Guide, the properties we need to develop as Teachers of God are enumerated in order to fulfill our function. The development of trust plays a particularly important role.

Trust is one of the pivotal points in the thought system of the Course. It is obtained by letting go of our tendency to control our lives piece by piece. Where our ego was running on auto-pilot, the Voice for God can direct us now every day and make it a unique gift to God and to us. By following this path we will understand more and more of his real nature. This kind of trust we will speak more about later.

10. A Mystical Path for the World

What the Vedanta is for Hinduism, the Tantras for Buddhism, Sufism for Islam and the Kabbalah for Judaism, can this Course be for Christianity and the whole world, a mystical path towards the experience of the absolute. It has Christian language, but it is not limited to Christianity. The course is unfathomable in its height, width, depth, and its effect. It transcends all human limitations in a completely sovereign manner. We have only just begun to understand a bit of it. It is quite simple and boils down to one decision for God. Those who are ready to follow the inner instructions in this book, will find themselves soon in another world in which they will be assured more and more of God's love and guidance. Their lives will be an adventure in which they will let go of their own convictions little by little in favor of the ideas given to them by the voice of God. They realize that real freedom can only be found beyond their human self-identity based upon separation and specialness. They recognize their true identity as the Sons of God, who live forever and are connected with everything that God created as part of Him. Outside of God there is nothing.

11. Jesus' Conversation with a Soldier

Mecklenburg, May 1945- WWII, on a path in a forest...

Heinrich- fleeing German soldier is talking with Jesus

H: "Am I dead now, Jesus?"

J: "No, you're not dead Heinrich. I'm just here to urge you to hurry up if you want to see your wife and your daughter."

H: "I have a daughter? And Erika lives? And you think the Russians are close behind me?"

J: "They will catch you, if you daydream further like this. It is time to run quickly now until the next road, where the last German truck will take you to the American lines. They stand now east of Schwerin."

H: "Thank you, I will rush. Yesterday we received the BBC news in a farmer's house. They said the Germans have killed millions of Jews. They have reportedly found thousands of deaths and even gas chambers in several concentration camps."

J: "And what do you think?"

H: "I have not really thought about it. We made our jokes about the Jews, but the rumors of gas chambers we did not believe. I had serious talks only with close friends, but I tell you, once you have found a true friend, he was already dead beside you. A short twitch and he was gone. It was all so sad. I think I could cry for the rest of my life. The cold, the hunger, and the constant danger! Hitler did not care about us; we were just cannon fodder for him. I slept three winters outside, wrapped only in my army coat, nothing else. Food was coming from time to time. I have seen the columns of Russians that we had defeated. After the great battles of encirclement in the beginning, an endless column was walking west, that stretched to the horizon."

J: "Did you see Jews in the East?"

H: "Yes often in small towns, at the train stations, rounded up by SS and Wehrmacht, poor and frightened people."

J: "What did you feel?"

H: "I felt pity. But only for a moment."

J : "And then? "

H: "I've swallowed it. Since then I have this terrible cough."

J: "And what were you thinking?"

H: "I did not want to know what kind of fate was awaiting those people. I assume it isn't a good one. And then I thought, if these wretches are not parasites as we have been indoctrinated over and over again, but just people, then God help us!"

J: "I assure you that they are not parasites, they are normal people, no different than you and your family. Something like *Übermenschen* does not exist. God has created all as one."

H: "If the Germans killed millions of innocents, then we are cursed forever."

J: "Even therein you're wrong. There is no eternal damnation for God. Even the Russians will forgive you, even faster than the British."

H: "Do you think? We have burned down the whole country."

J: "Have you killed civilians?"

H: "I shot Russians who had already surrendered. It went so fast and I thought 'What the hell? Just fuck it, I don't stop shooting now.' Once, a family was running into our fire on the main line. It was terrible to see children and women die."

J: "Can you forgive yourself?"

H: "How could I do that, but should I? Would you, would God forgive me?"

J: "If you are willing to take responsibility for your actions, then you will receive forgiveness."

H: "I need time. I think I'm getting mad. I have seen too much. And the pictures do not go out of my head. I want to shoot myself to have peace finally."

J: "What did you feel when you heard Hitler on the radio for the first time?"

H: "I felt scared."

J: "And what do you think now, was this fear justified?"

H: "Yes, when I think back, yes. But what could a poor boy do? "

J: "Trust your intuition in the future. And follow me. Then you will find peace. True peace is in God, not in death."

12. The Cosmology of the Course

God can only create like Himself. The extension of God into infinity is called creation in the Course. Therefore the world of space and time in which life is always limited, did not arise from the will of God. But only what God created is real. Since God is infinite, the world has no place where it could be. Only in the past it can abide, but eternity is forever now. But how did the world then come into existence? To this question there can't be an ultimately satisfactory solution, only an approximation. A central teaching of the Course is that ideas leave not their source. This means that no system of thought can leave or transcends its source.

A thought system of oneness must extend forever in perfect union with itself into infinity. A thought system of separation must teach separation forever and must split itself more and more into smaller and smaller parts. The world has evolved from a single idea of separation. The Course talks about this little crazy idea that spoke of separation and specialness and calls it ego. This idea sprang undetected through the universe. The Son of God listened to this thought and convinced him to ask his father for more than everything, namely for the favor of a special love. But God could not supply this pledge of his son because he loves all in the same way forever.

God had already given the Son all He could by creating Him as everything. The son felt as if He was rejected. And He no longer understood His Father. The unbreakable confidence of infinite peace and the boundless love of heaven fell apart in his perception. This disintegration of the original oneness into countless parts is called the *Big Bang* in modern scientific language. It is interpreted within the science community as an act of creation, not of destruction. Until now there is a pure understanding of a world beyond space and time and without separation in the West.

In other words, today's physics is finally beginning to discover a universe beyond the space-time-continuum. This world is a unified field where an instantaneous communication exists between all parts, what religiously speaking the "heaven" is.

After the loss of heaven, the Son of God fell into the world of time and space, being bound to a body, surrounded by other bodies. Then God sent the Holy Spirit to call His son home again. Jesus of Nazareth was the first person in our culture who recognized this spirit as His own and followed Him. Jesus became the Savior who opened the path for all the others. He is the older brother, whose resurrection founded the salvation not His crucifixion. He asks us to stop crucifying ourselves and others. He calls the crucifixion the last useless journey of the Son of God. It stands for any kind of sacrifice that men impose on him and/or others.

To see oneself and the others as a "body", that is ultimately what crucifixion is. If that's true, we have fallen deep indeed. We see each other only as bodies and do not know how we could see something else instead, for example, spiritual things. The course will draw us out of our depth all the way into heaven and in order to do this it asks a lot of us. It is suitable only for the strong in spirit, which means that it can be completed successfully only by those who are willing to ask God for help and also to receive it. That's why it is called, *A Course in Miracles*.

I want to make a statement here about the patriarchal language of the Course. When the course speaks of the "Father," the "Son of God" and "brothers", the Course uses a language that is oriented towards the unity of the Spirit, and does not refer to physical differences. This language is also used for healing. The old contents of Christianity were served as a repression of the feminine. It is used now for the liberation of all. The Course asks the student to see beyond the body. Like God, everyone is spirit and only spirit. The student just dreams of living in a body.

13. What are Miracles?

In the Course, the word "miracle" has a special meaning. The central idea is that there is no order in miracles. If a miracle should be possible at all, then it can change all things, how big or difficult they may look like. It's not about to change the world according to our own desires. Miracles, as understood in the Course, overcome illusions and bring us therefore closer to reality; that's why our miracles are not important in themselves. It is important, however, to recognize their source, which is far beyond any evaluation. Therefore, miracles are here not considered to be something special, they are, on the contrary, a natural process, because they represent reality within a world of illusions. They are expressions of a love that connects us all.

Miracles are an expression of life itself, as well as the voice that inspires them. As we said, miracles become the voice of the Holy Spirit and a personal guide of the student of the Course. The aim of the Course is an ongoing listening to this inner voice and thus the ability to be truly helpful.

Miracles should not be subject to conscious control. They must involuntarily since they follow a plan that we can not know on earth, due to the limitations we have imposed unto ourselves in this world. Miracles are the right of all people, for they help to cure a deficiency under which almost all suffer. They bring the giver and the receiver more love. They should not be used as a spectacle. They have no place at fairs, because they are played out in the inconspicuous, on an interpersonal level, in the world of feelings and thoughts. Nevertheless, prayers are important for miracles.

We have to ask for miracles, for they represent a communication between heaven and earth. They change time by shortening the timeline that extends from now until the end of this space-time continuum. In other words, with the help of miracles that are unlimited in numbers, we can return to heaven faster. They free us of the past and free our mind for the future. They testify to the truth. It does need faith to let them happen. Each day should be spent with miracles. They are part of the curriculum. They shift the awareness from the visible to the invisible and show the unreality of the physical plane. This makes them heal. They provide a service; they are an act of love and reassure donors and the recipient of the intrinsic value they both have in the eyes of God.

Miracles can unite the mind of a whole group of people with God. They show that the mind is the medium of truth and not the body. Miracles do need forgiveness. Without forgiveness they can not happen. Miracles create fear in those who are afraid of the light, because they believe to be guilty. Only when they realize they're innocent, can they let go of their fears of the light and surrender to it. Miracles give us the opportunity to heal, because we have introduced the idea of disease into our perception.

Everyone is responsible for his dream. Miracles assure us that we are a miracle because we were created by God and therefore can create like our Creator. Miracles can create a chain of reconciliation, which will when accomplished extinguish all blame forever. In this way, the apparent existence of three-dimensional space-time will be overcome in our awareness and a space will be created for the vision of the other world called 'paradise' in the Bible.
The atonement works in every moment and in all dimensions of time. Miracles represent liberty from fear because they are based on faith and they strengthen it. Miracles are a blessing. By them, forgiveness and renewal is coming from God through the miracle-worker to all beings. By this, God is praised.

Miracles should not inspire awe, because the children of God are as holy as their father. Miracles are inspired by Jesus. They give back to the mind it's inner strength, because it learns from them to think again in the right way. This means to think as God thinks. Miracles can never be lost, even if their effect is not visible yet. They can have effects far beyond the visible frame and the familiar environment.

Miracles try to bring what we have done closer to God's real creation again. They bring earth closer to heaven.

14. Miracles - Stories and Experiences

What is the meaning of miracles for our lives? Maybe stories can best describe this. These stories may sound unbelievable to some extent, but they all come from people I trust.

A Precognitive Dream

My grandmother dreamed 1946 of a day when she was driving around in the courtyard of her sister's farm with a horse car. In her dream she knew that her own house had burned down at this moment. When she told the rest of the family about this dream they just mocked about it. Then on Christmas Eve, 1946 the house burned suddenly. That was the worst time for that to happen. The Russians had occupied the country, everything was scarce, much was destroyed and my grandmother was a widow with three children. While the house was burning, the men of the village came running, shovelling the grain harvest of the year from the burning floor of the thatched hall house into the yard. They saved the harvest of the year and that was what we call a miracle in the Course. For the rest of the year my grandmother and her children ate stony, smoky tasting bread, which inflicted some damage to their teeth but they had to eat it. The moment of the dream really happened, she remembered it when she drove the horse car in her sister's yard.

She found another husband and rebuilt the house, which still stands today. The miracle was the fact that they were preserved, even in their darkest moment. As a child I always believed my grandmothers, who were cousins, who told me this and similar stories because I believed in the miraculous, contrary to the rest of the family. The dreary material world of the 60's in East Germany, which was regarded by the other as 'without an alternative' seemed too boring and insignificant to me.

Only later I realized that miracles require a completely different way of thinking. Miracles occur only when we are absolutely 'miracle minded' or when life has pushed us into a corner where we have to let go of control. Who wants that? To be a human being means to have control over one's own life and to defend it jealously against death, until God or nothingness snatches it back from him. Control is understood as life, loss of control as death. The Course sees this vice versa. For it, we live in a world of death, in the midst of a living universe, where all things are perfectly controlled by God and therefore by love. Since the identity of God includes His creation, which includes the knowledge of God and the understanding of his will. The truth is much different in the Course than we thought it was.

I once met a man on a train from Berlin to the north. The train was a half hour late in the station of Oranienburg. The man looked so mysterious, as if he came straight out of a movie. He sat down opposite to me. After we had looked at each other for some time, he said:
"The voice has already told me that the train will have a delay."
"What voice?" I wanted to know.

"The voice that always speaks to me. She said to me that I should sweep the stairway. But I said that I would miss the train. But the voice assured me that the train will be delayed and I would be on time at the station."
My curiosity was peaked. The man had a strange look. His eyes glowed inwardly in an unknown fire.
"Since when do you hear that voice?" I asked.
He looked out the window and was lost in thought for a while. "It was in the second world war. I was in a trench. In front of me were the Russians. We Germans were on the decline. I was the last survivor in our whole line of defense. Behind me there was no cover, far and wide. Only flat, icy Russian steppe. And yet I could not surrender. I thought the Russians would shoot me right away because there were no other witnesses. So I jumped out of my trench and ran away from the Russians. The Russians blasted out of all their barrels at me. The bullets whistled just around me

everywhere. And I cried all the time 'God! God! God!' The bullets did not hit me. I escaped. Since then, I hear the voice."

The Course both is a miracle. It is the rescue of the soldiers and his lifelong listening to the inner Voice for God, as the Holy Spirit is called in the Course.

Saved Twice

The following two experiences come from a Jewish scientist, pilots, and mystics, whom I want to call Alvin. I was several times with other friends in his log cabin on the Wisconsin River as a guest. We were all in Wisconsin in order to study the Course with our Master Charley of whom I will talk a bit later. Alvin had many stories to tell, of which I have chosen two. When Alvin was a boy of 7 years, it was around 1938. He boarded a train from Cologne to Berlin. He drove in a closed first-class compartment, which was actually forbidden for Jews. He was alone, trying to enjoy the ride. After some time the train stopped, and something happened that started like a nightmare. An SS-Standartenführer in a long black leather coat slowly marched down the aisle.

He read the number of Alvin's compartment, opened the door, and came in with great stride. He took off his hat and threw himself on the opposite seat of Alvin. The boy tried to be as normal as he could be and looked fixedly out the window. The SS officer began to take off his coat and gun and make himself comfortable on his bench. Then he said something quite unexpected, "This time you do not have a

Moses who can save you. Everyone needs to be his own Messiah." Al looked at him in amazement. The officer went on to talk about the Old Testament, which he seemed to know very well. Then he suddenly became personal and lowered his voice.

"Listen, I know you're a Jewish boy. You have to promise me to tell your parents what I will say to you. Do you promise that?" Al nodded uneasily.

"When you get home, tell your parents that they should pack their bags right away and leave the Reich the fastest way possible. You must flee to the west, not to the east. Will you say that? "

"Yes sir, I'll tell them."

The officer nodded. "It´s really getting bad here, you understand, you can not stay."

Alvin and his parents followed the advice of the Standartenführer and left the German Reich to emigrate into the U.S. The city of Cologne had invited him several years ago to an event for the surviving Jews of the city. It was the first time after the war he saw the city again.

Another miracle that Alvin experienced is one of the more well-known that Sai Baba is said to have effected. Sai Baba was an Indian saint with hundreds of thousands of followers, who was celebrated as an avatar and ascended master. Prior to the miraculous event, Alvin flew as a pilot with a small passenger plane over northern Nevada and lost in a heavy snowstorm orientation. The plain was shaking and he could not see anything, because his radar system failed. He had almost run out of fuel. That was it. Was there any other option left except to dive, crash, and die? Alvin had indeed one more action to take before giving up. For the first time in thirty years he asked God for help.

He did not have to wait long. A voice came out of the cockpit speakers. The voice gave him precise instructions for landing. He did not know where he was, except that he was far outside a populated area. Suddenly, what appeared was a runway amid the clouds and the wilderness of rugged mountains and snow-covered sand dunes. He brought down the plane safely and ran to thank the air traffic controllers of the control tower.

"Thank you for the help!" He said to the two officials, who were still staring stunned out the window. "You have brought me down here very professionally! We had run out of fuel. Ten minutes later and we would have fallen from the sky like a stone." These two officers looked at him in amazement.

"We did not have any contact with your plain, sir! You came out of nowhere. "

Alvin discovered later in Mexico a picture of Sai Baba, which was almost completely covered with ashes. This ash had the property to grow by itself. It was distributed among the followers as beneficent medicine. Sai Baba always seemed to materialize it from nowhere and to scatter it on the audience of his listeners. "That was the man who brought me down." Alvin said. When he asked Sai Baba later in India directly about the Airplane, he confirmed that he was the one who helped.

The next two stories are hard to believe by someone who has not experienced something similar himself or heard from reliable witnesses yet. The important thing is not to measure the message of this book on the credibility of each story. The stories cited here are still tame. There are many other experiences that are even crazier.

On a Desert Island

The following story was told by a friend who was a small, very fragile man with long hair and a soft breathy voice. He owned a small shop for health products and massages in Berlin at that time, near Oranienburger Street. He was spiritually, a very serious man and not a braggart. As unlikely as the story might sound, I didn't doubt for a moment that he was telling the truth.

"I flew to an island in the Pacific. From there I was transported by fishermen to another uninhabited small island. I told them to come back in two weeks. I wanted to spend time in solitude and meditation. When I had traversed the island, I realized with horror the absence of fresh water. How should I survive the two weeks without fresh water? I decided once again to look more closely. I searched the island and found in fact many large tree leaves, which were filled with rain water. I drank from the water and thought I could make it. Then I realized that this tree water developed an unfortunate side effect. My throat narrowed. I was breathing harder and harder. I noticed that the breath would soon completely stop. I was at that moment of course, completely on my own. I layed down on the beach and tried to calm down. My breathing was getting thinner. Finally, it stopped completely. I laid there and was not breathing at all. It was not pleasant, but not unpleasant either, just unusual. I could die at any moment, if I would panic or fall asleep. But as long as I laid still, nothing would happen to me. For me, a lot happened that night. In the morning, my breath slowly began to flow again." How he survived the rest of the time, I forgot to ask. Maybe he drank again from the leaves and started the exercise all over again.

Only Twenty Seconds

The following story comes from Andrew, a teacher of the Course, who lived in New York for a long time. At 9/11 he was with other brothers at Ground Zero and helped several people who were wandering around in shock. Many miracles occurred here. At this moment of deepest agony the gates of heaven were wide open and things happened that would not have been possible otherwise. Within a few years, New York City fell back into the normality of deep sleep though. Andreas lived there at the time when I visited him at the crossing of First Street/First Avenue between Uptown and Downtown, a neighborhood with alternative shops and cafes, where the ever-present scent of incense and pot announced an alternative lifestyle.

My girlfriend and I stayed right across from Andreas' apartment in one of the cheapest descents of the city. We stayed at the youth hotel of the Hare Krishna Temple. Because I worked for several hours during the days renovating the rooms, I could stay there for only twenty-five dollars a night; otherwise it would have cost sixty-five. My room was right above the temple. This meant that I was woken up every morning at 4:30 when the drum and the choir of the community were singing: "Hare Krishna, Hare Krishna, Krishna, Krishna, Hare, Hare. Hare Rama..." Andrew himself once had been a bigwig in the Hare Krishna ISKCON organization and could enter the hotel and eat breakfast for free. Once, for an hour, we joined a group of Indian dancing and singing monks of ISKCON, when they made their rounds in a nearby park. Andreas, a large athletic man in his sixties, is a great communicator.

He had the ability to connect with the people in the streets of New York and bring them into contact with the inner light. After such a meeting they found themselves in a different world than before. The following story took place in his youth. Because of the Vietnam War in the U.S. conscription, he was active in the late sixties and early seventies.

Andreas eluded the convening by changing his place of residence every two weeks, spending two years practically on the road. He acted here quite legally. He always reported the new address immediately to the city and the Army. But since the bureaucratic apparatus of the U.S. Army needed a certain amount of time to send the convening papers to the new address, he was always in a different place when they reached the destination.

He told me that he had only slept twice outside in these two years. Again and again the people with whom he had hitchhiked or who he met on the road had taken him home. With God, he did not want to have anything to do, except he trusted the universe that he would be taken care of always, which was already much more than many Christians are able to do. Once, however, it looked bad for him. He was in the middle of the night somewhere, knocked off in a lightless wasteland. Freezing rain soaked his clothes and he saw no more way to find shelter.

He was shivering and was sure that his death was imminent. He fell to his knees, looked up at the black starless sky and prayed for the first time since his childhood. "Universe, God, I'm dying. If I go somewhere, if there is another life for me up there, then please give me a sign!" He did not even ask for help. At this point of the story his voice always failed.

It took God only twenty seconds to respond! Headlights of a jeep shot around the next corner of the country road where he was. There were soldiers in it. The car stopped and took him with them.

From that moment on, he was in search for this God who had never let him out of sight.

When he got to know the Course and realized 'Yes!' to God, he was afraid. "I do not want to have to fight like Albert Schweitzer in Lambarene with the heat, the disease, and the mosquitoes, but if you want, I'll do even that." The answer of the Holy Spirit was the following. "You are only expected to live always in the passionate ecstasy of light and miracles. No other sacrifice is requested!" He happily agreed. Since then, he is a living expression of this order.

Life Without Anything

Another story comes from Victor, an Argentinian who teaches today in South America and in Spain the 'light food process'. I've heard his story from a close friend of his, who himself is a famous dragon painter.

One day, an inner voice told Victor he should stop eating. And he stopped eating. Later, the voice said also he should stop drinking. And he stopped drinking. He survived, but gradually lost all his teeth. Some time later, he felt a strange pressure in his jaw. They were new teeth coming out piece by piece from the gums and gave him a completely new set of teeth.

He was a passionate paraglider. One day when he was about two thousand meters high flying over Columbia and all of his ropes were cut almost as if a sharp knife. He dashed into the depths. He hit the ground in fast speed breaking many bones, but survived. The physicians in the local hospital inserted silver plates and nailed and screwed all fractures together. During this time, his body was temporarily returned to liquid supply. After a few months, he traveled to Barcelona and came to the hospital for investigation because he was not feeling well. It turned out that there where no silver plates on his bones, but a cheaper material. They took everything out, including the nails and he left the hospital as a healthy man.

The German movie, "Lichtnahrung" does not only talk about several people who don't eat anything for years, but also about a Sadhu, a holy man of India, who has not eaten anything for seventy years.

They invited him into a hospital for a two week investigation. They measured all his body functions. It was not clear where he got his fluid from. But the movement of fluid was almost like in the body of average people. Urine was produced for example, but was return to the circulation of the blood. According to the Hindu teaching, particular people are able to live out of prana, the universal energy, without further food supply.

Contact

My friend the painter, told me about another friend of his, who works as a healer in Buenas Aires. He heals with stones. One day he was contacted by a tribe of the Amazonas in the rainforest. These people asked him to visit them. He had no idea, how these people, who never have been in any town, could know about him, who lived several thousand kilometers away in a different world. He had two meetings with them. The first one was at the edge of the rainforest.

The elders told him they were watching him for a long time and had decided to give all their wisdom to him, because they wanted to leave the planet soon.

He agreed finally even though this burden was not easy for him. The second meeting the tribal people asked the sixty year old man to visit them in the forest. He took his plane from Buenas Aires to Rio. There, he had to change to the inland airport. After another flight, and a long trip with the local Amazonas ship, he took a canoe which brought him three days up a stream deeper into the territory. After finding a gap between the branches on the river bank, the boot driver let him get out and said, "If you want to find the tribe you have to go three days south. You really want to do it?"

The stone healer took his stuff and walked into the forest, for three days south. Then he found another river and decided to turn left. After another day walking he found his friends. There were sixty people on this trip. Ten of them were elders. They gave him all their wisdom and knowledge, including an initiation and said, "You can do with it, what you want. Our job is done."

The healer traveled back to Buenas Aires and wrote a book. This book he printed twenty times and gave it to his friends. Now it is their decision what to do with it. He returned to his former job of a healer. There are many stories from Argentina, Mexico and other countries that question our point of view of reality. But for now we made our point.

To understand what the Course In Miracles means with the term, 'miracles', we have to move away from the physical and ask ourselves what the Course really wants to accomplish.

It wants to reunite the Sonship. The miracle is a moment of communication between two persons or better minds.

Because of that the miracles can be totally inconspicuous. Often only those involved in this experience acknowledge it. But a 'physical miracle' can be important for those who still have to learn the lesson of the reign of spirit over matter.

Firewalk

Anyone who has ever been involved in a firewalk can see this with one's own eyes and feel it with one's feet. I was once invited to a firewalk in winter. I tried to resist it but I had to follow the third call and drove with my friends to a country side close to Dresden. It was negative fifteen degrees Celsius. The fire had consumed a high pile of beach tree wood and consisted now of four meter wide circles that was made of embers and ashes. It was so hot that it almost burned my eyelashes.

And still wanted all the twenty gathered people walk over this with their naked feed. We had the order not to resist the fire with mantras like "cool meadow, cool water" but to let it go through our system. So there I was on the edge of the glowing fire.

I was standing on the snow on the coldest night of the winter. My feet were burning on the cold. In my head, two thought systems battled with each other. One said: "You are totally crazy. What are you doing here? You will die." And the other said, "Just go! Others have done this before. You are safe. Don't wait longer!" Finally I walked. I wanted to be the first. I sensed my feet. They felt cool in a comfortable manner. What I had feared, this terrible burning on the feet, was caused by my hesitation and was overcome by my walking. The others followed.

The second time, I felt safe and was not really concentrated because the other had walked several times already. Therefore, I received a light burning. The third time, this burning was healed, it went away. A man carried his wife over the embers. The leading woman said last time a woman walked in nylon socking over the fire without burning them. How could that be explained? Our group seemed to have created a protection filter between our feet and the fire.

We have already talked about the power of a shared intention which leads to the writing down of the Course material. Therefore, a firewalk should only be done under the guidance of experienced leaders and never by a single person alone. It is a classical example of how Jesus wants miracles to be understood. Not as an act of magic and self elevation, but as the outcome of a shared prayer for healing and release.

Mary Between the Sea Mines

My grandfather was a protestant pastor in town in the north of Germany. During WWII he was writing letters to the young guys of his community who were on the front line. One of these letters remained mysteriously visible on the cylinder of the typewriter until the time when I received it. I could read the whole short comfort letter, although my grandfather had used this machine for thirty years. He was part of the German Lutheran Church, which was resisting the claim of salvation of the Nazi-regime.

During the war, the official task of my grandpa was to run through the streets of the town during the bombing and to report all strikes to the Fire Department. This was an extremely dangerous task. One time he came home crying, "They hid my church!" The grave of the burned down St.Mary's Church was standing until the sixties, when the Communists blew it up for no reason. The tower of the church remained until today. As a sea-mark it was untouchable even for the Communists. After the war, a veteran of his community came to my grandfather and told him he had converted to being Catholic.

"Why is that?" asked my Grandpa.

"It was during the war. Something happened that I can't forget, and it changed everything. I was a submarine captain. We were trapped within a field of mines. There was no hope to escape it. I looked out of the window into the dark water, where death was waiting for us everywhere. I prayed for help. This was the last option. Then suddenly a shining woman appeared in the water. I could not believe my eyes. It was Mary, the Mother of God. She showed us the way. I let the machine start and I followed her. She carried us slowly through this labyrinth of deadly traps.

The mines appeared from time to time like black demons in the dark blue light of the deep water passing slowly. I informed our crew about what was happening, that we followed an appearance of Mary through the field of mines. A loaded silence spread out, a silence filled with tension, speechlessness and hope. This was going on for a half an hour. Then we were outside. Nobody cried out of joy, because we had to remain silent to avoid being sensed by the underwater microphones of the enemy. But we fell into each other's arms and cried. Mary had led us out to safety. It was clear for me to convert to the Catholic Church. But Mr. Pastor Steinbrecher, I still have to thank you so much for the guidance and love during the war."

My grandfather could understand the young man very well. In 1944, a well-known and honored Jewish doctor of the town died, who probably had an 'Aryan' wife.

My grandpa walked as the only priest behind the coffin through the empty streets of the nightly town.

The people were watching him behind their closed windows, lit by candles and admired him for his courage. They believed he would be the next victim of the Gestapo. But the British took the town just fast enough to save him. My grandparents did protect a Jewish woman on the church properties in the countryside for a while. When it became too dangerous, they sent her to other people in Berlin. What are miracles? When will we fulfill our task? Does everyone have a task? Yes, sure.

The *Old Man*

When I was told that my grandpa had died, a light went off in my life. I have searched for this light everywhere since then, but could not find it. Only when I found the Old Man could I see a reflection of this light and a way to follow it. Before that, I had the terrible feeling of being trapped in a hamster wheel. In the summer of 2001, I visited three similar cities that were Lion, Vienna, and Praque. I saw the same scenes all the time; houses from the 1880s, hills with trees, and nothing new under the sun.

In Prague, I spoke at least once with a woman, who had known Kafka and his father and also the story of the famous journalist Egon Erwin Kisch who was searching for the Golem, the industrious, magical clay man launched by Rabbi Löw under the roof of the Old-New Synagogue. He found only pigeon poop there. After this trip to Prague, I would meet the Old Man, an teacher of A Course In Miracles, I knew, and I perceived with wonder and anticipation that someone was drilling already a hole in the top of my head, preparing my mind for the vastness of the cosmos.

When I finally met my master, a stout man of medium height in his seventies, he immediately said to me, "You have to choose!" That was not exactly what I wanted to do at that moment in my life. I had just found a new job in Berlin. Should I give it up in order to devote myself entirely to the studies of the Course? I knew I was very lucky to find such a teacher.

This like an old friend. A few weeks later I was out of the job and had abandoned my apartment in Berlin. I had reluctantly accepted that there was a plan for me, which was not made by me. I thought until then I was an insignificant speck of dust among all the millions and billions of people and that was not true.

Now I was told that I had been located, so to speak, on a Divine GPS and found myself safely on the way home. Many wonderful spiritual experiences and coincidences showed me that I was actually in a different frequency or even world. The next seven years I devoted myself to the study of the Course in a camp that was run by a kind of brotherhood. Miracles were very common there. But the real miracle was the communication between all of us and it was much easier than the outside world. If you thought about someone, he or she might come around the corner or phoned you. If you needed something, it was provided very quickly. Something similar I experienced years later on the Camino de Santiago in Spain, where even the weather was directed very precisely according to our needs.

The Old Man or Charles had gone into the Marines, the ground forces of the U.S. Navy, after America had been shaken by the Japanese attack on Pearl Harbor. Charles fought with the American troops from island to island through the South Pacific. In Okinawa, his best friend died in his arms after he was caught by 'friendly fire', fire by their own troops. He saw this as a fundamental unfairness of life on Earth. After the surrender of the Japanese Emperor, he was among the first American troops who occupied Nagasaki. The destruction in the city by the atomic bomb put his joy about the American victory to an abrupt end and plunged him into deep despair.

He went to the hospitals of the city, and looked at the misery. As he had witnessed the ruthlessness of the ground fighting in Okinawa, he did not doubt the necessity of the American High Command to force Japan to surrender with all means in order to spare the American troops a loose ground offense on the main island. Then he recognized the hopelessness in that situation. For him, the entire human situation became as hopeless as Nagasaki. As he walked in agony on the mountain slopes around the city he met a former enemy, a soldier of the Imperial Japanese Army. He was not less desperate than him. These two men became friends without words. The Japanese invited Charles to a tea ceremony.

In this ceremony he experienced for the first time the power of forgiveness. This experience therefore did determine the further course of his life. First he became a businessman. He had constantly so many ideas that he did not know what to do without getting lunatic. Alcohol was his salvation up to the seventies. Not until it was too late he could admit to being an alcoholic. He said about this time that he drunk himself happily into liver cirrhosis. Finally, he was admitted to the hospital. Since liver cirrhosis was not curable, he was taken to a room for the dying. That was irrevocably the end of his drinking career. He knew that he had to die within hours.

What happened then appeared a figure of light. This entity asked him if he wanted to have a second chance. He said "Yes!" and he was healed. When he came out of the dying room, the doctors looked at him aghast.

The next day he left the hospital although doctors protested. My master henceforth worked in a twelve-step program of Alcoholics Anonymous until his ultimate enlightenment happened. While this was unfolding he had such a terrible headache that he asked for an ambulance to bring him to the hospital. During the trip, he hit his head against the metal wall of the van, in hopes that the pain would go away. Then a voice said to him, "You are in a process." "Thanks for the information," he answered. In the hospital they found nothing like a tumor. Later, when he was alone in his room he had the feeling that the whole universe was collapsing into him. He hid himself under his carpet. In the morning he was fully enlightened. He knew there was no world. But who would understand and believe what he was saying?

He waited long in vain for a way to tell others of his awakening. Years later as a friend of mine visited his house to see his daughter, he asked Charles out of curiosity who he was. My friend saw the whole universe, stars, and galaxies emerging in the open spirit of the Old Man. He did not hesitate to become his first student. Many stories like this could be told, but in this book. As the Old Man the Course in Miracle was shown, he looked at the book and said, "If you have that, you do not need me anymore." But his students convinced him to teach the Course, and that's what he did for the rest of his life. Miracles happened with such ease in his presence!

In the early days of the Brotherhood, stories occurred like the one of Henryk. He drove at high speed on a one-lane bridge and suddenly a truck appeared in front of him, and it was obvious that is was going to crash into him within a second. There was no way to dodge. He looked ahead to his certain death. At the last moment before the impact, Henryk closed his eyes but nothing happened. When he opened his eyes again, he found himself 150 meters further at the next crossroad. The next morning the Old Man said that Henry was brought back from the dead. Miracles don't need to be so dramatic. But we have to want them. They release us from our thoughts and ideas, by which we have locked ourselves away in a cage. Therefore, the Course offers freedom. As the Bible says, "Your entire burden cast onto him!" If we learn to trust God in the big and small things of life and give up our worries we can already be happy here on earth.

15. Jesus' Third Conversation with Lucifer

New York City, Central Park, January 2012.

Lucifer: Black coat with hood, black beard, black eyes.

Jesus: Blue-eyed and blond with a beard and long hair in Afghan coat.

L: "What the hell happened to your huge return, Jesus, the infamous Second Coming of Christ, in thunder and lightning, and the roar of fanfares dripping with blood, with falling heavens and the earth opening up full of fire, streaming from the deep? And in the midst of all this chaos the luminous Christ who floats delicately down from the clouds, with blond hair and bright blue eyes as you show even now as a nice hippie camouflage in Central Park. And we have further the idea of teaching. You wanted one half of humanity to gather to your left and send them after a brief trial forever into hell, into the eternal fire, where I would have to torment them with pitchforks and sulfur, because they did not meet your high demands. And the other, these holy benefactor and hypocrites, the pious and righteous, you wanted to gather on your right and take them with you to heaven. And now all this is cancelled. You return only as a book, as a self-help book, as there are already thousands. That is what is left from the great Second Coming of Christ. "

J: "Yes, the vengeance of God is cancelled. What bad news for the devil. "

L: "And with the Second Coming, the hope of salvation is gone down the drain as well. The world still rotates on its slow way around the old sun and the people are still waiting for you."

J: "Not in vain. You said it already, I returned as a book or better as a message. Who always strives, we can redeem, said Goethe already. Therefore, we need to convince the people that they must want deliverance to obtain it. I can´t do that for them. And you strive diligently to distract these people. My message to them on the other hand builds a bridge from the sleep of darkness towards the bold awakening in the light of God."

L: "Yes, it sounds quite nice, this plan. And all of this should occur without sacrifice? How ridiculous. This heaven that is supposedly open to all, but still nobody can enter. This vision of another world that you speak of all the time, who do you think obtained it, really? I know hardly of anyone. Your words sound wise and as sweet as honey. But what has really changed since the Course is published? Just have a look at your Course community. They are deeply divided, enemies, and split into sects.

The first publishers earned a fortune and thus were hatred by many until the old man withdrew that copy right from them. And Gary, this hero who receives allegedly ascended masters in his living room and writes one book after another, scolds in each book anew about the old man or 'Master Teacher', as if he was the devil himself, because he was not received as a master by him but like an idiot. Wise sayings I see, but no deeds. Again, nothing new under the sun, as the preacher in the Bible had already said a long time ago."

J: "Like always you hit the sore spot, Lucifer. Everything should have been much better. But the real thing is once again slipping through your fingers, because you are looking in the wrong direction. You are searching for errors because you made a mistake yourself. He who seeks will find, as you know. In reality, everything is going according to plan, if we see it or not. And concerning the vision we've made a few adjustments. "

L: "What do you mean?"

J: "We have added some exercises that will be conducive to the attainment of the vision."

L: "What do you mean 'we'? I thought you had concocted the Course all alone. "

J: "The textbook was compiled by a group of four spirits. These spirits were Meister Eckhart, Mary Baker Eddy, Meher Baba and I. The first twenty lessons of the exercise book were designed by some Zen masters of the Chan-period in China. We all had a lot of fun together. "

16. The Development of Trust in the Course

A student of the Course can have trust in the world again. He can be sure that all things will serve him, because his life is no longer subject to the control of the ego. Now he has invited another power, the Holy Spirit, into his life. He learns to perceive his life in a way that strengthens his trust in God, rather than to undermine it. He knows that he is always under the God´s protection, because he lives and acts in his service. To learn to trust in His power, rather than in one's own is the goal of mind training of the Course.

At the beginning of this mind training it seems as if the life of the student is falling apart. It seems as if things he thought he needed for his safety and joy were taken from him. In reality these things never served him well. He just had bound himself to them, trusted them and thus lost sight of where his real security lays. Now he must learn to sort out all the things that are not helpful. What he has learned so far must be applicable to all situations, if it is true. All things, encounters will now be helpful as God sends them.

It can look as if the student must sacrifice his own best interests on behalf of truth. But that is quite impossible. He has not yet realized that his whole life is filled with worthless things and not things that have real value. God never ask for a real sacrifice.

There will also be times of peace, in which the student is easily carried along as on angels' wings. But from time to time he will be challenged again.

Ultimately, the student will be called to serve more and more to the inner voice. This may cause anxiety, for he can have the feeling of losing the inner freedom, because he is now under a higher order.

At the end of the development of trust, lies the state of completion. It this state he listens always to the voice of the Holy Spirit and doesn't need to be corrected or to any inner guidance. The peace of God is the reward for his confidence. Fear will no longer be a part of his life.

17. The Perception of One's Neighbour as Healing

The Course focuses on the perception of others as the 'Way of Salvation'. If we want to see our brothers separate from us, we deny them the salvation to which they are entitled as children of God and we will therefore see ourselves as unredeemed and as in one body. As a body, we will always make the experience of dying, which is the fate of all bodies. However, if we see our brothers as one with us, a new perception comes to us, the Vision of Christ. This is a holographic view of the world in its unbreakable unity of the Spirit. This mental change can not be brought about by the student alone. It is the greatest of all miracles and is awarded to those who requested the redemption for themselves and everyone else.

18. Forgiveness as the Answer

This world was made to give reality to the idea of separation. But now under the auspices of salvation it becomes a teaching institution of healing, union, and love. This world was never a fact. Since God has answered with the plan of salvation to it the world has already passed in reality. She is only a distant memory now. The positive purpose of this memory is the complete forgiveness of God's children of themselves, each other, and their Father. This seems to need a lot of time and the support of many teachers of God.

In reality, the son only needs to forgive himself, for there is no other.

If the forgiveness is complete, the world has served its purpose and will disappear from perception. After that, the real world will appear for a short time, which will contain all the loving thoughts that were given by anyone in this world. After a final blessing to this highest form of perception, this will disappear into the final awakening to reality. Thus the Son of God has returned into his Father's arms, and the journey that never really happened is forgotten.

19. New Hope for the world

Right at the beginning of the teacher's handbook is the offering to give life a new meaning. So far, the future Teacher of God has used the world to hide himself from God and demonstrate the reality of separation. Now for the first time the door to a different decision is open. The student can look at his thought system without fear now, as an alternative has been shown to him. Until now he has built and defended an illusionary self. With the beginning of his training as a Teacher of God, he agrees to abandon this old self step by step and to claim back the memory of his true Self.

He will become a new hope for the world. In a circular learning situation, the idea of death appears to contain the only hope of escape. He discards the knowledge of a real way out. When the Teacher of God fulfills his mission, to pass this teaching onto those whom he was sent, he learns his own lesson and finally accepts the atonement for himself, which means nothing else than accepting his own innocence and that of his brothers.

The decision to be a Teacher of God brings forth a deep initiation inside the spirit of the student. This soon changes their lives and their experiences in the world. In earlier times, such an initiation was only done by secret brotherhoods on hidden places in a dramatic culmination of the revealed ideas in the symbolic and condensed form of a ritual. Things are different today, and yet in some ways, still the same. Only the dramaturgical aspects of the initiation are now left to life itself under the monitoring and care of the Holy Spirit. Nevertheless, this initiation that follows along with the decision for this Course is one of the deepest of which we have knowledge. By the publication of the deepest mysteries contained in the Course, a lot more people can do this step today. The need for it lies in the desperate situation in which the world finds itself and there is an urgent need for a solution. The world needs quick help and the teachers of God are the means to bring it about.

20. The Life of the Teacher of God

How can we imagine the life of the Teacher of God? In many respects it resembles the lives of others. But it is just as Jesus promised in the Course. His forehead is smoother, because he worries less. He learns more and more to trust. He realizes that there is actually someone who cares for him. First, however, when the new student deals with the lessons of the Course, he will notice that more anger is rising in him than before. This can be caused by an inner resistance to the new system of thought brought by an uprising of old emotions that have been supressed until now.

Suddenly the ego is confronted with an alternative with which it did not have to deal before.

II. To walk the Path of Love

1. The Problem

Only by the perseverance of all successful fighters of God, this phase can be overcome. This is called cleansing and forgiveness in the Course. This phase can take years, and you should be patient with yourself, but it can take much less time, because it takes just one decision for God to achieve a breakthrough to inner freedom.

After this phase, the ascension into the light begins. This is the time of service when the student follows the instructions of his inner intuition, because he realizes that his joy is to be helpful. At the end of this step, lies the accomplishment of complete forgiveness. The spirit says Jesus has already decided when this will be. We need not to worry, we may miss the target. Our enlightenment is inevitably. We go back to God and the whole world is waking up with us. And we don't need to correct anyone, nor do we preach because those days are gone. Correction is for us, who walk this path, not for others.

When we are in search of love and peace, our basic problem is not the lack of love outside of us. Love must always first be found inside of us, before it can be mirrored from the outside. But if we do not feel love for ourselves in us, then we have to think we are not worthy of it. If this problem is resolved or better if this feeling is healed, then we will have no trouble finding love inside or outside of us. The Course offers us new ideas about who we are and shows us the direction for our search for love and also where we can find it. But we must be willing to change our mind about all things. This is not easy. Most of us would rather be right than happy. This confession is not made by many, but they defend their thought system, like their own lives without ever honestly investigating what they are defending and why.

2. Love is not Outside

In order to follow the Course, we must consider some basic assumptions as a possibility, and open ourselves to them, at least tentatively. One central idea of this teaching is mentioned again here. The source of love is not outside of us. Furthermore, nothing exists outside of us, but only as a reflection of an inner state. This is the hardest idea to accept. In the east this change of mind is called the direct path. This Indian path of Hindu Vedanta calls for an identification with the self-awareness which includes all things, and is without limits. This changes everything. If we change our mind, the world is changing.

The world we see is not our source. The source of the world is in our head or better in our mind. If this is true, we still hold the power in our hands to change our lives and even the world. We have indeed made the world we dream of, but we did not create ourselves. There is a source in the universe that created us and this still cares about us. We have a memory of this inner source in our hearts, but are afraid of i, because we believe it to be guilty. Our guilt is only imaginary, although it can appear be very really in the world. But the source of our identity is still present as an inner voice. This voice can teach us to love again and to find happiness if we follow it. It will always speak for forgiveness because this is the way of salvation.

3. Forgiveness Brings us Back to Love

With forgiveness we rise above the clouds of guilt and fear and wake up in the light of reality. The first step to a new way of life in love may be the following confession:

I do not know the answer, but I can ask.

We do not even need to be sure of who or what we ask, it's just important that we are inwardly prepared to listen to an inner voice, which is not identical with our mind. Everyone has had the experience that the world reacts to the internal state. If we are happy people smiling at us on the road, when we are angry, we are jostled and collect all the bad energies that surround us. How is that possible?

4. All Things are Connected

Quantum physics has found another world. This is a world in which everything communicates with everything at the same time. This is already demonstrated by the EPR paradox, encountered by Einstein after calculating the formulas of Plank with two colleagues, but this he could not believe. This experiment shows that when a particle is broken into two parts and both halves whiz in the speed of light in opposite directions the two still react as one particle. Even if the two particles are millions of light years away from each other and one of them is deflected, the other responds in the same instant, with the identical but opposite movement. This experiment, also known as the quantum-entanglement, gives us a key for our Course, because it transcends the laws of time and space. It shows the world we see is not real, because divided particles react still as one. Why don't we?

5. The Power of Ideas

Some people use this law of duplication for magic. The modern magic has taken this idea as its own. The whole universe is the product of one particle, the so-called Hicks-Quant, which was created just after the Big Bang and then divided into trillions of other particles that make up our universe formed by time and space. Therefore, these twin particles can be located anywhere and could affect the whole universe. Also in the theory of magic, all events have a twin aspect, a kind of blueprint in the invisible worlds. A shaman could see in a vision that a flood would destroy his village, for example. This would be a blueprint in the invisible realms of reality on the way of realization in the visible world. He could now, in order to protect his people, build a model of his village and flood this model, to anticipate the flood. If he was successful the outer part of this twin is thus already accomplished and the coming flood is skipped. On the other hand, one can create a blueprint of a desired event so it can be shaped in the visible world. The ancient cave drawings that show hunting scenes, may constitute such a hunting magic. But we are not here to follow the path of magic. That does not need to be done anymore because we are partakers of a greater protection, one bigger than we could ever dream of. The path of magic can reveal, however, that this world is made of ideas, just as Plato has already claimed in his allegory of the cave.

Our next step can then be, 'I now let go of my old ideas and open my mind to new ones'.

Other ideas lead to different results. We do not know these other ideas, because they come from outside of space and time. We therefore open our minds to the inner teacher, because the solution does not come from us, but for us.

6. Change of Mind as Miracle

Any major change of mind is a miracle. When we want to wake up from this dream of isolation we need to ask for miracles. Fortunately, miracles are natural, because God always takes care of his children and this world is just a dream. Miracles occur when we let go of control for a moment in our mind. Miracles can be frightening for those who use this world to hide from the light that shines around them. That's what most of the people do, who live on earth, otherwise they could not stay here long. But if someone starts to follow a spiritual path, he changes his mind, and he realizes that there is nothing he wants to hide or wants to keep for himself.

This Course is devoted to forgiveness. This can lead to very practical steps. For example, we can write down the names of all the people against us and whom we have something against. Then, we try to realize that love can only come back to us, when we have forgiven all of them, whatever they may have done to us. Sure, there will be certain people we never want to forgive. We therefore begin with the smallest resentment towards those who we still love and work our way from there to the most difficult ones. In this way, we learn how to forgive and what forgiveness can do for us. We should bring this difficult soul to work and assure ourselves that this is just our own dream. These people could only do these things to us because we have somewhere, somehow asked for it. This is a hard thought to accept. Sometime when we fall in love with being a victim or being in pain, we are here because we wanted something different than the serene joy and complete innocence of heaven. We are now asked for the willingness to forgive all our brothers and sisters.

7. Love can not be Contained

To feel the love in our hearts, we must expand it. Love can never be kept. We have to extend it in order to have it. Therefore, we can not really take love from the outside in, as we have tried maybe many times. Love comes from within, because God is inside and there are only reflections outside. We are so to speak lost in a hall of mirrors. To want to correct the quirky images of the mirror, that will only consume unnecessary time and never get us out. We are still the masters of our fate, because everything we want is still in us. But we have robbed ourselves of the inner strength and power, by denying us the life and sparing it with ourselves. By refusing the natural desire to love, for some reasons we have lost sight of love itself. Can we now at this moment start to give ourselves away? We can pay attention now to all that is within our reach. To give attention means, to be aware, and to not to fall asleep again. To grow more and more aware is the task of a lifetime. It must be practiced again and again. We should extend the love of our hearts to all beings, if we want to free our hearts. The more we give this love, the more we will feel it and the more it will be mirrored back to us.

8. Melting

If we are no longer 100% identified with the body, we can do the work that we are asked to do. This work includes the reunification of the body with the whole universe. When this is done, there is nothing left to forgive or to attack or to defend against. The body is experienced as a unified space, combined with everything. Our will should be united with the universe at all times. We will then be able to receive messages from our higher self and serve all living things that touch our lives. Love will not be searched for outside, but will be given as part of ourselves. It will be a never-ending wealth in us. We can now say, "I give myself away to find my own."

III. The Course in Life

1. Following the call

Now you have heard about the offer of God and that the world is only your personal dream. Everything is still perfect, because your dream could not change the truth about you. On the other hand, this also means that your attempts in creating something new, you have failed. This is why you're not really who you appear to be or who you defend.

Your identity as a physical being that is separate from the rest of the universe is not true. Furthermore, the world you see around you has no meaning, since it reflects only the facets of your fragmented identity. But how can you take new courage when you have understood all these things and have accepted them? You live in a world in which there seems to be so much suffering, but it is actually going on only in your mind. You fight for surviving and you build an identity that has only meaning for yourself. And all your sufferings and efforts end all in vain. No, not really. Everything you have done so far has led up to this moment. And now you have the opportunity to decide again for the voice of someone different who will give you happy dreams in exchange for yours. These dreams you will dream about not alone and the burden of responsibility will no longer be on your shoulders. The meaning of any day will be understood as a gift, because it will be no longer artificially grafted onto it. Meaning comes out of the question, "Does it serve love?" If so, that's good. If not, then it is meaningless. We live now a life of service, a service to God and our brothers and sisters. This may sound like an exaggeration because maybe our lives have not so terribly changed. But not what we do in detail is important here, but for whatever reason we do it. If you have given your life to God, then you will serve all things in a very different manner than before. But even this is only a beginning. Better dreams do not concern us here, but the awakening from all dreams does. You can already see now, that you never left heaven. If you accept this idea, your entire perspective changes completely. Then you do not need to defend yourself against the world, because you know that it ended a long time ago.

You can now completely rely on God who safely guides you through this remembered world. He leads you to brethren who need your light and to those who awaken you through theirs. How will it be after the awakening? Where will we find ourselves without this world? The Course speaks of the forgiven world and of its disappearance into the infinite light of God. That's the goal. This is not the end of life but the beginning of real life. We can create worlds over and over again. And we've always done it. There are many universes. The number of adventures we can undergo is infinite. Boredom is a privilege of earthlings who are sitting on their couch watching TV. Their passion has long been buried under a blanket of cowardice. That's not what God wanted for us. The life we are leading on earth is so dead that you can not imagine the real universe. What is it that makes this world seem so dull and dreary? Apparently it is the compacted matter that is completely opaque.

2. Dealing with Guilt

In reality, guilt is the denial of the Voice for God. That led a great part of humanity live in darkness. It's the life in separation which is the opposite of a life in complete solidarity, as it is lived in the universes of the real world. How can this error ever be fixed? The Course is one of the answers of heaven to the call of help by many people. It only talks about the important things and wasting no time. Buddha once said the following, "Whoever stands in a burning house, should not ask about the cause of the fire and the nature of the burning materials, but should be only concerned about one thing, leaving the house." He spoke of the awakening.

The Course remains true to this claim. That's why it always points towards forgiveness. Why is forgiveness so important? Because we are responsible for the world we see. Buddhism does not go so far, usually. It talks of "mutual conditionality". This means that no one created the world, but that it was made out of an infinite chain of circumstances. The responsibility for it therefore remains in the dark. The Course does not want to make anyone guilty, but teaches on the contrary that sin is an illusion. Before we can enter the peaceful land of innocence, however, we must take total responsibliley of the guilt in our minds. That includes the guild reflected by the world. We have made the world get rid of that guilt. Now we should take it back and hand it over to the Holy Spirit. We must have the courage to raise our self-defense and drop all our justifications and allow us to be completely guilty for a moment. Only if we are willing to do that, we will come to enjoy the forgiveness of God. In this sense, the confession of the Catholic Church lies in the right direction. God does not forgive, because He has never condemned, says the Course. But one must first reach this place where there is no condemnation. He who feels guilty needs the assurance of forgiveness. That is why it is so important that we forgive one another. Only then can we be confident that even God has forgiven us. Who does not forgive, has to feel guilty, because the guilt that he sees in the world must be his own.

How can the course help us now to leave our fortress of attack and self-defense? As long as we are in this fortress, all our blame must appear as irrefutable and totally justified. It takes a miracle to change our mind about it. But even a miracle needs an inner preparation, called 'cleaning by Jesus'. Love can not penetrate a scared or hateful mind. The Course therefore works with our beliefs. Once we realize that our thought system stands on unsustainable ground, we can give it piece by piece to the Holy Spirit. Only when we have questioned it, the light of truth can penetrate this construct. The Course not only takes apart our ego thought system, it also gives us an alternative at the same time. This new thinking is a translation of how God thinks into our space-time reality. There are now two systems of thought in our mind. The conflict seems to be more intense than before. In reality, it was only raised into awareness where it can be cured. The practice of the Course therefore needs patience and trust. A failure can only occur when we give up halfway. But anyone who walks home with the power of God on his side to a place must be successful. The road will be completed faster and safer if we forgive all those who we have some resentment to right at the beginning. We have to do that in the end anyway. We can specifically use the fourth step of the twelve-step program of Alcoholics Anonymous. The strength of this method lies in the fact that it gives us back the responsibility for the wrong doings of others. Thus we rise above the life of a victim. Similar things can be accomplished in *The Work* by Byron Katie. The Course has specific exercises for forgiveness. Other effective methods rise out of our minds and above the battlefield. They are meditation and the practice of awareness.

3. The Course and Meditation

Information about meditation has been written a lot, but not all practitioners have been successful. This is only if we want to describe success as an entrance into a spread peaceful awareness. When the mind is silent, it can turn to awareness as it's true nature. This awareness will grow in us if we give it attention. But even if we will repeat the lessons of the Course incessantly, the dawning of awareness does not take place automatically. What can we do?

To be successful, one must meditate and avoid external frustration. Some things need to be considered. Once you have sat down with your back as straight as possible, you should first breathe deeply a few times and look around the room. Then you should use the body scan and ask yourself how you feel today. Also, it is important to make clear to yourself why you want to meditate today, so keep the motivation for daily meditation always fresh. The real meditation is performed by beginners by counting the breath. With every breath, two numbers are counted, 1-2, 3-4, 5-6, 7-8, 9-10, and then again from the beginning. It is essential not to try to actively change the breath nor the state of mind, but to leave it the way it was.

When our mind has become silent we can hear the messages of the Holy Spirit better. We know at any moment where we have to be and what we should do. It is not as if a permanent sacrifice for others will be required of us, as we often fear. The Holy Spirit knows us better than we know ourselves, because it is our own whole mind, as stated in the original text. Therefore, we will take care of ourselves better than before, enjoy walks in nature and ensure a healthier diet. Why is forgiveness so important? To understand this we must bear in mind again the view of Cosmology expressed here. God is considered as the source of all that lives. That's why we are a part of Him. This means that each of us is unique and that God includes but all beings as part of himself in his mind. If we exclude someone who is part of us from our mind and want to see him as separate from us, the awareness of our identity must be lost. When we forgive, we reunite our minds and we remember that all things are part of us and we are part of God.

4. The Kabbalah

In Kabbalah, it is assumed that the separation from God has really taken place. The Son of God, referred to in Kabbalah as, 'Adam Kadmon'. According to this teaching, he is eventually fed up in receiving free gifts of God. The seeming undeserved gifts are in the myth of the Jewish mystical tradition called the *Bread of Shame*. Now Adam needs help, after he has thrown himself out of heaven. The Kabbalah gives him this ladder that leads back to heaven. The means for the ascent is a reversal of what Adam has done at the *fall*. Now, the Kabbalist is called upon to act rather than to react, thus creating in an active manner and so recoup heaven piece by piece. The invocations of the names of God work with the connecting lines of the Kabbalistic Tree of Life or also called the 'meditation of transmutation'. This works with groups of three Hebrew letters, and in some exercises that are part of the repertoire of this system.

In this Course we are not trying to find the way back to heaven nor earn it back. Heaven is priceless, it can only be given, received, or remembered. Therefore, the Course says that although we have thrown heaven away, it has been preserved for us, because we have nothing to buy it back. Also, we were not able to ever leave heaven, because there isn't a place without God. The great Kabbalist, Isaac Luria developed a theory saying that God withdrew himself from a part of the cosmos to give space for the illusion of space/time. This process was called by him tzim-tzum.

The Course rejects this point of view. Here the world is merely an unreal curtain that each one of us has pulled before the truth in order to forget heaven. By choosing the awakening, the life of the student as a whole becomes the ladder back to heaven. In order to recognize what is already here, the mental change is the only thing needed. The truth, however, can not be touched or changed by the world.

5. A Moment is Enough

All that is necessary for a return to heaven can be accomplished in an instant. It is the desire to return, which accomplishes this journey home with the help of God. In time, this may take many years because it is difficult for the human mind to abandon his usurped ability of judgment. It seems to be a sacrifice for something unknown and feared as well. Forgiveness ends this deception. With forgiveness, we let go of the past and therefore, our identity. One realizes that he can not judge, he is no more than an ordinary man. In our civilization, the development of judgment is seen as the path to maturity. Following the Course is the world we see ready to raise a judgement.

Who adheres to the judgment of the Holy Spirit can learn a different way of looking at the world. This is called the 'process of a silent meltdown'. All things are allowed to be as they are and to return to us so that we can see what they are, which a part of us is. The salvation sought by the Course is nothing more than the recognition that all things are inside and none are outside. This awareness is 'heaven' as Jesus says in the Course. How can we allow this meltdown to happen or even accelerate it?

The following exercise is inspired by Michael Barnett.

Imagine that your arm is a cloud of energy. Attempt to feel the vibration. Forget for a moment that your arm is made of matter. If you have achieved this, let the energy that surrounds the arm sink into it, even if it feels uncomfortable. Let these external energies penetrate the arm. Let the arm be raised to a new level of vibration. The external energy will allow the arm to swing in oneness with the universe. It is basically pure light. What you also will feel as your resistance are all the hidden blockages to the free flow of energy. These blockages will be dissolved slowly by the light.

If we have understood the universal applicability of this process only once, we can use it to make the whole body vibrate more and more with the universe. But what really happens is the other way around. The world returns to you. The energetic pressure decreases and ceases ultimately, because you no longer insist on that almost everything is outside and almost nothing inside. Everything slowly becomes a part of you. In this exercise, forgiveness is therefore applied. In this way, we are again an open inviting system that brings its home always with it wherever it goes and invites all beings to return home. This is the function of the Teacher of God.

6. Jesus' Conversation with a Priest

In a small village church, in a dark cemetery, on a night in November.

The old retired priest closes the church door and sets off to the neighbouring territory.

Jesus appears before him, bathed in radiant light.

P: "So did you come?"

J: "Yes, I finally came."

P: "It took a long time, very long."

J: "Time seems to last forever, when you're in time, I know."

P: "How do you feel about me? Did I pass or fail? "

J: "You have passed. You are your only judge. You will have the opportunity to see your life again with all the consequences of your deeds for others."

P: "I am afraid of that."

J: "Do not worry; this will be an intense but brief experience. And you'll be able to feel all the love that you have brought to others, as well as their disappointment about your failures. However, the harvest of your life is rich beyond measure. Then you will understand how grateful I am for you. "

P: "Thanks, it's good to hear that."

J: "You have been my voice; you gave me hands and feet. You have brought me to the poor and the lonely, the proud and the fearful. You have built a warm place in this village, where nobody knows about hope, except for the young people who want to go away without knowing a destination that will not disappoint them. Come home now, my brother, to the house, I have prepared for you before the beginning of time. Let us celebrate the feast of homecoming, the feast with which the dream of separation will end. With you all the children will find themselves at home. The Father's supper is open to the sinners and the righteous, because God knows them all just as his children and their dreams are only foam for him. None of you could change like when He was created. After the party we will sing the hymn again, praising the Father, the Creator of all universes from eternity to eternity, who knows each of his children, as if they were his only children and give them all the gift of everything. The old song that we have always carried in our hearts, the song that is nothing more than life itself, is indescribable ecstasy and yet so filled with profound peace that this is unfathomable and without any end. Welcome brother!"

7. Two Exercises in Acting

1. Imagine first your finger is completely empty then your hand and piece by piece your whole body. Imagine all things as empty, the chair you are sitting on, the floor on which the chair stands, the desk, the furniture, the walls of your room, etc., until you look at the earth and all the heavenly bodies as empty. Then let your attention wander from the inside of your body to the outside. Find your spirit wherever you go with your attention; in the body, outside the body, in the coach, in the soil and again outside. Establish a space of awareness that pervades all things. Now let all things melt into this space of vision by relaxing your eyes.

Stay faithful to this exercise, until you begin to see in another way.

2. Let all things come to you unfiltered. Open your awareness to all dimensions, angels and beings, and be the empty space in which all things may enter without resistance. Be the black hole through which this universe of separation will ultimately return to the Father. Go with the gravity and find your way home.

8. The New Beginning

Be yourself.

Jesus speaks again, "I did not come to change you. I would rather give you the courage to be yourself. What does it mean to be you? Apparently you are trying constantly to defend yourself against your perception of the things that are beyond your little world, against other people and what they could want from you and against other ideas that might threaten your identity. This identity I have always questioned. Through my crucifixion and resurrection I have shown that the life of the children of God can not be attacked. Only in this world you seem to be vulnerable.

This is so because you have made the world in order to give your limited identity that is bound to a body any meaning. You're here because you're afraid of your grandeur. Littleness is your way to deal with the guilt that you feel deep in your heart, since you believe to have separated yourself from God. My message has always been based on your holiness. What God has created can not change and God creates only perfectly. This means that you are connected to everything and there is nothing outside of this set. This is the peace of God and he is enrolled in it your heart, under all of your fear and guilt. But as long as you are projecting your dark feelings and thoughts over and over again into the world, healing can not happen. Now it is time to open your mind and heart for healing, because the old ways no longer work. This is an invitation to a new beginning. God has given you back to yourself."

9. Lucifer

"Today I want to talk about the opponent. He can only be outside of heaven. Heaven is still as it always was, just you are missing there! That's why I'm still here to call you home. Your life is your response to that call. You can delay your return home, but can not prevent the final outcome. No one can claim your soul and snatch it out of my hands. Lucifer seems to have a great power in the world, greater than God. People worship him and bring him blood and other offerings; above all else, they sacrifice him and their inner peace without getting back anything real. And yes, indeed, they feel his dark power surrounding them, like a colt black blanket. Is this proof of the existence of a devil? There seems to be forces and energies that resist God, but they only have the power that the people have given them. And believe me, these Luciferic forces believe to serve God by planting negativity and pain in a tepid system to push it into a decision that will in the end always be made in God's favor . But you decide alone about who the leading force of your life is. How do you do that? You can do this by demonstrating what you believe, less from words but by your deeds, by your life lived. In that sense, Lucifer is a part of your mind, a voice that you invited to throw out the voice of God.

You wanted to forget heaven. Why? You wanted more of God than anything in order to have the privilege of a special love. God could not give you this for he loves all beings equally. So you have pushed away the love of God in the belief that the whisperer, the ego, or Lucifer could offer you more than God himself. But all that he could offer you until today was separating, cold and painful. What is Lucifer? He stands for a certain kind of thinking that is based on separation, a program that you can turn on when you want, but that has no power without your power. You need not turn it on. In every moment you are free to decide for God. Therefore God must eventually win, because he really is infinitely greater than Lucifer.

All you have to do is land at this moment and to demand the freedom of choice back for you."

10. The Path

"Look around you. Stop wanting to do something. Nothing is necessary to improve yourself. You are already perfect. Why would you need to do something? Is God far away and therefore must a ladder be built back to his throne? Who should build this ladder? You maybe, with your understanding of God's love? Certainly not! The ladder is not about you, it's for you. It is already given. It used to be equated with my cross. But now I tell you that everything you need to step through the gate of heaven is trust. All your spiritual knowledge, leave behind you. Trust is already yours, after you've learned that God is with you; you just have to apply it today, right now.

The best thing you can do now is to open up to what is here right now. And that's a lot. First of all there are your sensations. Then there is the interior of your body. Does it feel as empty as the outside space? If not, you still have to do some work. And this work consists of nothing else than you being able to be moved by the cosmos, until your body vibrates in the same frequency than the space around you. Does that mean that empty space vibrates? Yes, everything vibrates, everything dances, everything sings. Just give up your resistance against the vibration of the outside and let first a small part of your body be moved by this external vibration such as an arm, and later the again become a part of the universe, you realize that you have always been a part of it. I call that the peace of God. How can you live this peace? You live it by seeing it in each and everyone. Let this peace radiate from your heart like a light, so that it makes your chest wide and warm. Then see this shining in other people around you. By seeing it in others, it will make it even more your own. You can also identify with the emptiness in all things and in yourself and transform it into a unified space. This will give you the freedom to transcend your body without leaving him. By identifying yourself with space, you make room for God and love. Bodies can express love only imperfectly. Your mind is already one with everything. All you have to do to extend this love is to think a loving thought. It is in your mind where love will either be retained or extended from. If you extend it, it becomes yours. Hold it back and you lose sight of it, because you have contracted yourself and love is expansion. This simple clarification should open you up to the way back to the Father. Stop reading, get up and follow your path. Your brothers and sisters are waiting for you to go ahead, so they may follow you as you follow me. I will guide you home, by serving them. In the end they will welcome you in heaven and you will realize that only you have believed to be here."

Books by Peter Bernhard:

"The Gates of Mary Magdalene" A Spiritual Adventure in Berlin

"What Jesus really thought" This book describes the original teachings of Jesus Christ. His goal was to show a path of liberation to his followers. This was different than the teaching of the Church about him as a savior. Jesus was a Savior because of his teaching. This books provides a step by step process of learning and liberatio

„The Course Of Miracles" The Zen Teachings of Jesus. The path of A Course In Miracles, with other stories of students, Lucifer and Jesus.

In German:

„Der Kurs der Wunder" über eine neue Art zu Leben und Christus nachzufolgen, für das dritte Jahrtausend.

"Die Pforten der Maria Magdalena"   Einführung in die gnostische Lehre des Märchens "Eisenhans"

„Christsein in der Matrix"   Besser leben in einer unwirklicher werdenden Welt.

„Das Evangelium der Katharer" Wie würde ein Evangelium aussehen, das keinerlei Angst vor Gott erzeugt?

„Die Katharer" Begegnungen, Liebe und Abenteuer in den Bergen Kataluniens.

„Im Westen ist das Meer noch tief" Das Abenteuer der Selbstentdeckung auf dem Jakobsweg.

„Christliches Mantra". Durch ein betendes Leben Sinn und Freude finden.

„Mit Crazy Horse im Schnee". Eine bewegende und abentheuerliche Erzählung über die Begegnung eines Mannes mit seinem Tod.

„Ethik und Integration" Wo steht die deutsche Gesellschaft heute? In welche Richtung müssen wir uns bewegen, um den Herausforderungen der Zukunft gerecht zu werden und die vielen Fremden zu integrieren?

„Was Jesus wirklich lehrte" Die 24 Erkenntnisse, die Jesus gelehrt hat, um den Frieden Gottes zu finden.

"Wir leben alle in Gott", Die verborgene Botschaft des Johannesevangeliums

„Die Allen der Kindhei", Gedichte über das Sein

Weitere Empfehlungen:

„Praxis des Herzensgebet"s, Andreas Ebert, Peter Musto, Claudius, München, 2013

„Unterweisung im Herzensgebet", Emmanuel Jungclausen, EOS, St.Ottilien, 2008

Other Authors on the cutting edge of the Christian new paradigm: Matthew Fox, Richard Rohr, Carl McColman, Cynthia Bourgeault , Paul Selig, and many others.

www.ingramcontent.com/pod-product-compliance
Lightning Source LLC
Chambersburg PA
CBHW022342290526

45786CB00014B/2368